THE
POWER
OF
URGENCY

THE
POWER
OF
URGENCY

Playing to Win
with
Proactive Urgency

William Keiper

The Power of Urgency

Published by:
FirstGlobal Partners LLC
7119 E. Shea Boulevard, Suite 109-177
Scottsdale, AZ 85254

For more information about FirstGlobal Partners, visit:
www.firstglobalpartners.com

Creative collaboration and introduction: Steve Chandler
Editing: Chris Nelson
Cover design: Brittany Alloway

ISBN 978-0-9849893-6-2
ISBN 978-0-9849893-4-8 Electronic

Library of Congress Control Number 2013940895

<u>Dedication</u>

for

Werner Erhard

An innovative thinker and leader, for a lifetime of proof that creativity, originality, boldness and courage matter—for your inspiration.

TABLE OF CONTENTS

Acknowledgements

For inspiration and support in the creation, execution and completion of *The Power of Urgency*:

> Steve Chandler, Chris Nelson, Brittany Alloway, Dr. Tamir Mosharrafa, Dino Babers, Wolfgang Koester, Dick Wagner, Jim Manton, Phillip Sassower, Andrea Goren, Jeff Holtmeier, Brett Keiper, my talented daughters Natalie and MacKenzie, my brilliant son Austin, and my fabulous wife Pamala Wright.

For direct and indirect contributions to and influence in the development and growth of my own power of urgency:

> Werner Erhard, Eckhart Tolle, Ralph Waldo Emerson, Dr. Albert Ellis, Larry Wilson, Jeff McKeever, Gary Liebl, Jock Patton, Jim Armstrong, Steven Forbes Hardison, Marty Wolf, Doug Goodyear, Errol Bartine, Jan and Tom Neely, Landmark Education, my mother Mary Parsons and my beloved animal companion, Baxter.

For award-winning and powerful images in *The Power of Urgency*:

> Jean-Louis Blondeau/Polaris Images (Petit on Wire), Charles McNally (No Trash), Bob Coglianese (Secretariat with Ron Turcotte), Roy McKeown (Snowy Sheep), Matthias Just (Airliner in Clouds) and others as credited.

Introduction

Lighting Your Own Inner Fire

by
Steve Chandler

When I first met Will Keiper I thought he had a bit of a problem. He wasn't a very good compromiser.

His preference was to *challenge* "go-along-to-get-along" company cultures and people. He was a man on the move and he sometimes came off as impatient. Some called him "brutally honest"—with the emphasis on the "brutal" part.

He would call it getting to the "obvious truth."

I later learned that what he had wasn't a problem at all. He had a special kind of objectivity and sense of urgency that was his alone. It was how he knew to be most effective. He preferred *results*—and rapidly.

It was clear he had found amazing strength and enlightenment on the other side of his warrior's sword. He had found his true calling as a genius change-agent-for-hire specializing in *very* rapid reversals of fortune.

From failure to success, from stuck to moving, from broke to prosperous. He could go into a company, bring his own brand of applied urgency to its most challenging problems, turn things around for the better—and leave before they knew what hit them.

Don't you wish we could all do that? Or, at the very least, have access to Will to come in and turn our own problems around that quickly?

Prayer answered! This book is proof that you *can* bottle this stuff. At least Will Keiper can, because as far as I know only he understands how to do this. I've spent my life studying systems that work to change businesses and lives. There aren't many that work, but this is one that *does*—maybe even the *best* one.

Why can this book give you the best system you may ever find for solving your biggest challenges?

Because it is the fastest.

If you can choose between a system that works when applied over a long period of time and one that works *right now,* which do you want?

Me too.

This book first makes the point that the power of urgency is known to all of us. We can reference it. We have all had situations wherein we had no time to think and plan, where we simply had to respond with the highest energy we had. Later we basked in the afterglow of amazing results.

This thought rose up: *Hey I didn't know I had it in me.*

Then, maybe years later, it would happen again. Emergency-level crisis and massive, inspired personal action taken in response. Usually extremely bold and surprisingly clever. Remember those rare moments?

But, as Will points out here, these events are all driven by external circumstances. We are challenged. We have nowhere to hide. We respond.

But what if we could turn this ability on and off by making a proactive decision to engage it? What if we could bring the urgency with us into situations of our *choosing*? What if we could elevate our consciousness into that *supermind* state we're all so fleetingly aware of?

And that's the very ticket. That's the lightning in a bottle that's been caught here for everyone to learn to use.

Will's stories and examples are wonderful. And what I enjoy the most is that he so obviously *lives* this stuff. He gives us his own story of a boyhood challenged by constant moving from town-to-town, never being able to feel settled and secure. Skills came from that. Adaptive skills that he later transformed into positive tools with which to serve others.

Now he has simplified those tools for each and every one of us to learn to use.

Why engage the *urgent situation/inspired response* only when the externals are bad? Why save that hidden bravery and creative genius for the worst of occurrences? Why not gain control of it and bring it to whatever we choose to solve? On our own timetable!

Of course, as Will points out here, we can't do this all day long with every little thing that crops up. This would exhaust us. We must choose our most opportune targets, achieve them, then rest a bit and choose others.

In his essay "The Energies of Men," the great philosopher and psychologist William James put it this way:

> Everyone is familiar with the phenomenon of feeling more or less alive on different days. Everyone knows on any given day that there are energies slumbering in him which the incitements of that day do not call forth, but which he might

display if these were greater. Most of us feel as if we lived habitually with a sort of cloud weighing on us, below our highest notch of clearness in discernment, sureness in reasoning, or firmness in deciding. Compared with what we ought to be, we are only half awake. Our fires are damped, our drafts are checked. We are making use of only a small part of our possible mental and physical resources.

Most of us can relate to his observations in that we are usually living our lives half-awake, with our fires damped. Until a big enough crisis appears—and then watch out for our magnificence! Watch out for our startling resourcefulness! Watch out for the fire!

This book solves that issue. It is not a meditation upon the power of urgency. It is not a psychological thesis full of good ideas (well, actually it is that, but it is also more than that). This book was written to give you *access* to the state you're in when you truly rock.

And for that I am feeling a huge amount of gratitude for my friend and colleague, the author William Keiper. His first book, *LIFE Expectancy: It's Never Too Late to Change Your Game*, was a bold wake-up call. It sounded a valuable alarm.

But this book is even better, because it gives you access to a tool you always had but never knew you could control.

Now read it and let your life, and your work as a part of it, change for the better.

Steve Chandler
Phoenix, Arizona

PART ONE

Discovering the Power of *Proactive* Urgency

1

<u>High Wire, No Rope</u>

Given his incredibly dangerous position, he was probably insane and likely to die within moments.

It was impossible to look away.

Although it was difficult to see him clearly from street-level because of the distance and the early-morning mist, the people looking up at him were riveted. The sight made some of them sick to their stomachs.

The man had longish, ginger-colored hair and wore what appeared to be a dark robe. High above the streets of Manhattan, he was flat on his back looking up at the sky. A long pole was lying across him and one leg was casually dangling below the level of his body.

The wind was blowing, there was no net below and he wasn't tethered in any way.

His improbable resting place was the mid-point of a slightly sagging, three-quarter-inch cable strung between the rooftops of the twin towers of New York's World Trade Center. The cable was precisely 1,368 feet above the onlookers—a bit more than a quarter of a mile.

Man on Wire.

Philippe Petit was not the least bit disoriented.

He was deliberate, calm and focused.

His appearance on this particular wire was neither random nor impulsive. Nor had anyone forced him to be there. Although this was an extreme showcase for his talents, he had accumulated years of professional experience on a variety of wires—both high and low—in preparation for it.

He had dreamed, planned and practiced to be in this precise place.[1] At this moment though, he was no longer *considering* it or *thinking* about it or *hoping* it would happen.

He was *doing* it and he could not possibly have been more committed.

Some onlookers said he looked as though he was dancing on the wire rather than walking. He moved with seeming ease all the way across the two-hundred-foot span between the rooftops. But reaching that destination was not the finish of this bizarre feat. It was just the opening act of a forty-five minute performance.

With the police shouting at him from both ends of the wire, he lightly stepped forward and then quickly back. He made a full turn and danced away in the opposite direction. No one dared chase after him.

Based upon his obvious command of the situation, he was clearly experienced, but he was also drawing energy and confidence from someplace else. Wherever that place was, it was making him smile.

He had tapped into a dimension of his being enabling him to be as urgent as the circumstances demanded. It wasn't mere *thinking* in the usual sense. At that moment, he was singularly focused on the achievement of his objective by trusting in his deeper *knowing*. He was harnessing the best of his personal power in the service of his goal, and was accomplishing exactly what he intended. He was getting results that were simply impossible for anyone but him.

But you can imagine that the people far below saw what he was doing as being well on his way to fulfilling a death wish.

© Blondeau/Polaris

But then we do not typically set our goals with the clarity that he did.

Nor do we often become as single-minded as he was about achieving what he had determined was his most important objective.

We do not, for the most part, even *attempt* to access the state of mind he was relying upon at that precise moment of truth in his life.

Nor do we typically manifest the kind of commitment that he obviously had, for perhaps decades, ahead of those awe-inspiring moments spent on the highest of high wires.

"Without the Rope."

In a dramatic scene from the Batman movie, *The Dark Knight Rises*, this clarity of choice about commitment is played out in a similar fashion.

Bruce Wayne is confined in an underground prison with only a distant patch of sky overhead offering proof that there is a way out. He attempts to scale a wall to escape from the prison while tied to a rope that provides a measure of safety should he fall. After several failed attempts it becomes clear that although the rope is saving him from death, it is also keeping him from freedom.

A fellow prisoner offers Wayne the seemingly nonsensical advice to pursue escape *without* the rope. He realizes that Wayne—by trusting the lifeline of the rope—is short of the full commitment required to complete his escape.

Mr. Wayne is faced with a stark choice: the possibility of a life of freedom which requires him to risk death—or the likelihood that even a valiant effort with the rope attached will keep him confined as a prisoner for the rest of his life.

Ultimately he accepts the fact that the safety represented by the rope is the very element keeping him from reaching his goal. He decides to hold nothing back; he goes all-in and leaves the rope behind.

Unsurprisingly, Batman lives to fight another day.

Proactive Urgency.

***Proactive urgency* is purposeful, insistent, committed action pursued with a passionate edge.**

In this book I refer to proactive urgency variously as pro-urgency, urgency-by-choice, applied urgency and conscious urgency. In doing so I am contrasting it with the fight-or-flight type of urgency that instantly—and automatically—seizes us when we are confronted with a crisis or emergency. This latter type I refer to as *reactive* urgency. Just ahead in Chapter 2 you will read more about the differences between the two.

The *passionate edge* of proactive urgency is engaged when you put more of yourself into something than is necessary to accomplish it.[2]

It is cool, clear, energetic and sustainable passion in the pursuit of something important in your life—something that, when achieved, will be game-changing for you, your business, your family or your community.

Philippe Petit and Bruce Wayne (and his well-known alter ego) offer examples of acting with proactive urgency that may seem extreme in terms of *our* typical challenges, and they are.

But the truth is that when you harness the power of urgency, proactively, you can tap into inner resources that will enable you to transform your work and your life.

Your Discomfort Zone.

Creating with proactive urgency does not require a daily confrontation with a "live free or die" choice. But the preceding examples suggest that to find and access your greatest personal leverage you must enter the promised land of your discomfort zone.

When you do, you enter a space where you can tap into your own sense of urgency in the conscious and passionate creation of your future. This is where you turn away from passively doing what you have always done or reactively accepting whatever comes your way.

Here you can ignite the parts of you that have become hidden, lost or numb. Entering your discomfort zone enables the engagement of the passionate edge I refer to above. You can use that edge as a tool for reaching the work and life objectives that you have determined really matter.

As you will see, acting with pro-urgency is life-enhancing, not life-threatening. When harnessed with commitment and clarity of intention, it is a force with which you can create almost immediate transformation in the service of your most important goals.

The purpose of this book is to show you how to discover or rediscover and consciously direct your power of urgency to make your life better, no matter the circumstances of your past or the potential challenges—and fears—you may face in the future.

Urgency Rule #1

Proactive urgency is purposeful, insistent, committed action pursued with a passionate edge. It is an activist choice to access your deepest personal power for the creation of almost immediate transformation.

2

<u>Reactive Urgency – Fight or Flight</u>

A sharp contrast exists between reactive and proactive urgency.

Understanding the differences provides insight into the extraordinary value awaiting you in your application of calculated, proactive urgency.

Instantaneous Readiness.

Reactive urgency is powerful, efficient and effective. It typically arises in response to a confrontation with circumstances that have (or appear to have) the potential for inflicting significant harm.

In this response mode, some of your body's most sophisticated systems immediately and automatically propel you into a state of laser-focused attention. Surviving the threat becomes your exclusive objective and you have no choice in the matter. In these situations your body is instantly turbocharged. You are compelled without hesitation into immediate action, whether that's staying and fighting the threat or getting away from it.

How does it work?

A significant perceived threat immediately mobilizes two key delivery systems in your body. The sympathetic nervous system controls bodily responses using nerve pathways. The adrenal-cortical system uses the bloodstream.

The triggering of these two rapid-delivery systems represents the full engagement of your fight-or-flight response.[3]

When this happens, your physical response to the threat is catapulted to a high level of intensity. Your bloodstream is automatically flooded with powerful hormones and other chemicals. Among these are epinephrine (adrenaline) and norepinephrine. These push your heart rate up and constrict your blood vessels, which immediately causes your blood pressure to rise.

The blood supply to the muscles in your legs, arms and hips, and to the motor and basic functions regions of your brain increases. Your breathing speeds up in order to supply greater levels of oxygen to the blood and to increase the pressure and speed with which it is carried through your body.

Just this part of the process creates the potential for certain kinds of extraordinary physical performance that typically would not be possible.

At the same time, your blood thickens, increasing the number of red cells carrying oxygen, white cells that fight against infection, and platelets that can reduce potential bleeding. The thyroid gland stimulates metabolism and secretes endorphins to act as natural painkillers if required.

In short, your body immediately brings to bear its most vital resources for a genuinely important objective: your survival.

You have become intensely alive and ready for action. No matter your age, gender, shape or physical conditioning, your body has become optimized for fighting or fleeing the threat.

In this primal, priming process what role is played by reason?

Imagine seeing a toddler in the path of an onrushing vehicle. If you stop to estimate the speed of the vehicle and how far away you are from the child, and then calculate how much time you will need to push the child out of the way, the damage will already be done. A reasoned response to an immediate physical threat will almost always be dangerously slow.

Though your resources for logical decision making have a role in reactive urgency, it is limited and secondary. This is why the automated response systems of your body don't give you the choice to rely on your brain for a rapid first response in these kinds of situations.

"I'm Not Really Here"

Another potential automatic response to fight-or-flight circumstances is "freezing"—that is, remaining near the threat but not actively responding to it in any way.

If it works it is a wonderful choice. If not, freezing will likely eliminate any chance of recovery or escape. Consider the misplaced and unfortunate choice made by a deer caught in the headlights of a vehicle accelerating toward it.

Even in the absence of a clear and present physical threat, we sometimes tap into a light version of coping through "freezing." Our specific or even non-specific anxiety can make us break out in a cold sweat, feel nauseous and cause our heart to beat like a bass drum. But rather than fighting or fleeing we sometimes choose a form of freezing called *avoidance*.

"I am so stressed, I can't get out of bed. I'm just going to lie here and die." The latter part of the statement isn't true, but it conveys the message clearly enough. It is a choice made to avoid confronting discomfort or fear by staying out of the view of perceived "predators," at least for a while.

In such moments it can seem as though we prefer suffering over taking the very actions—sometimes quite simple ones—that could provide immediate relief.

Giving Up Your Power.

It is common for higher reasoning to be overwhelmed by threats—real or imagined.

As to the latter, Mark Twain once said, "I've been through some terrible things in my life, some of which *actually happened*." We often and without thinking give imagined threats much more power than they deserve. Even the mere accumulation of day-to-day stressors can pave the way to feeling overwhelmed to the point of opting for avoidance. If you need a reason "not to" you can always find one.

Outside elements frequently have very little to do with how we feel. When acting rationally, we know that the suffering we endure is almost always due to the biases and skewed interpretations that are unavoidable consequences of our subjective assessments—what's going on *inside* us. But the course of least resistance is to attribute our distress to external causes.

Marcus Aurelius eloquently summarized it: "If you are distressed by anything external, the pain is not due to the thing itself, but to your estimate of it; and this you have the power to revoke at any moment."

Distress and Eustress.

Another way to think about proactive urgency versus automatic, responsive urgency is to consider the spectrum of stress with its twin poles of distress and eustress.

Distress is almost always associated with negative situations. When we are in extreme distress our bodies prepare us to fight, to flee, or to appear incapable of a powerful response.

Its counterpart is "eustress," a term coined by endocrinologist Hans Selye, a pioneer in the study of stress.[4] He defined eustress as a *positive* response to an external stressor. The degree of positive response will depend on an individual's location, feelings of control, and the timing and relative desirability of the stressor. Selye believed that eustress was related to desirable events and situations and could actually *enhance* functioning rather than degrade it.[5]

He concluded that the body cannot automatically distinguish between distress and eustress. A distinction between the two is dependent upon your subjective perception of the stress as good or bad, and your consequent attitude toward it.

Studies have demonstrated that the amount of personal control you feel over a particular stressor will actually affect your body's chemical response to it.[6] This means that an identical stressor can be viewed by different people (or the same person at different times) as relatively good or bad along a spectrum of potential perceptions. What seems to be a great situation for you could represent a crushing blow to another.

Reactive urgency occurs automatically in response to feelings of distress arising from events over which an individual feels no control but is drawn into a panicked search for a way out. Its counterpoint—proactive, applied urgency—is a positive response to stress, whether generated by internal or external events. The positive perception is *selected* by the individual who decides to pursue an objective with a meaningful commitment and persistent effort.

Proactive urgency is the use of urgency as a powerful tool, purposefully managed, to help you reach your most important work and personal objectives.

Not in a Hundred Lifetimes.

The following true story perfectly illustrates both ends of the urgency spectrum: automatic urgency working for the benefit of an accident victim, and the deliberate, applied urgency of a medical professional.

Jimmie Lee Clayton,[7] a twelve-year old Kentucky boy, was playing in the high rafters of a tobacco curing barn when he fell onto an exposed, upright eight-foot-tall post. The velocity of his fall drove the post all the way through him, side-to-side, and left him suspended about four feet above the ground.

He was in an unimaginable position: completely skewered through the middle of his body and unable to move. He was frozen in place—but not by choice.

This freakish accident had an even more unlikely aspect. Despite his situation, Jimmie Lee was still among the living, not to mention lucid and able to speak.

His body had responded instantly to the threat of almost certain death. All of his automatic protective processes were triggered and fully engaged in preserving his life for as long as was possible under the circumstances.

Jimmie Lee's friend immediately called 911. When asked to describe the situation, he said, "He looks like one of those pieces of party food on a giant toothpick." The paramedics arrived and saw that his friend was correct. They immediately determined that if the post was removed from the boy outside of a fully-equipped trauma center, he would quickly bleed to death. Instead, they chain-sawed through the post on each side of him, thereby separating him from the top and bottom portions.

They left about six inches of wood sticking out from either side of his body and secured him in the ambulance.

One Foot in the Comfort Zone.

The proof that this bizarre incident had happened was soon under the intense gaze of Dr. Tamir Mosharrafa and his emergency room trauma team in Lexington, Kentucky. Dr. Mosharrafa was a third-year general and plastic surgery resident who now found himself responsible for a life-or-death case that, as he told me, "Most medical doctors would not see in a hundred lifetimes of practice."

Dr. Mosharrafa couldn't quite believe the grotesqueness of what he was seeing, but at the same time he felt prepared to take the first steps in treating this young patient. He found himself in motion, totally focused on a comprehensive evaluation of the situation.

He wasn't conscious of it at the time, but he was calling upon all of his education and training, his experience as a doctor (limited though it was) and his unique gifts and talents as a human being. His four years of medical school, one year surgical internship and three years of residency had prepared him—as much as anything could—for the moment at hand.

He was also accessing a storehouse of knowledge and experience he couldn't attribute to specific education or experience. These important resources were served up to him from his subconscious in a way that fit perfectly with what he consciously knew. He was accessing his full complement of personal resources for everything that might be relevant to saving Jimmie Lee's life.*

"I had been taught that anxiety is the enemy of effectiveness. I wanted to make calm decisions about the course of treatment based upon as much deliberation as time and the patient's condition would permit. I couldn't believe how calm I actually was," he told me, "and at the same time highly focused, energized and prepared to act."

He wasn't sure where the words came from, but he looked at the boy and said, "You are going to be fine. We have a few things to do before we figure out how to remove the post, so let's get started."

He explained to me, "In trauma situations, there are typically more similarities than differences. I couldn't allow the sensational character of the patient's predicament to keep me from doing what I already knew to do. I looked for the indications that I recognized as comparable and familiar in managing his treatment."

The starting point was tending to the patient's ABC's. Airway: Is the patient's airway secure? Breathing: Is the patient breathing spontaneously? Circulation: Is the patient's circulation unimpaired? The ABC checklist represented the same routine he would initiate in any trauma situation.

---

* See Chapter 8: *Consciousness–You Know What You Need to Know.*

For Dr. Mosharrafa these familiar steps allowed the treatment to begin in *his* comfort zone. But he knew he couldn't remain there for long; he needed to determine how he was going to remove the post.

A Hand Saw.

With Jimmie Lee stabilized, the strategy for removing the post was discussed by the surgical team. Rather than risk further damage by pulling or pushing the entire piece of wood out from one side or the other, they decided to open up his midsection and saw the post in half.

To do this they utilized a flexible wire bone saw (a gigli saw), which they placed under the post. Dr. Mosharrafa gently pulled the wire saw back and forth under the post until it was in two chunks. The pieces were pulled out of each of his sides (like pulling arms out of sleeves one at a time).

Miraculously, the post had not damaged any of Jimmie Lee's major organs, arteries or bones. He was kept under observation at the hospital for a few days and then sent home to his family.

The Undeniable Power of Pro-Urgency.

As Dr. Mosharrafa related this story to me, I was struck by the power created at the intersection of the automatic, urgent physical responses of the young boy and the alert readiness and deliberate but equally urgent efforts of the young trauma surgeon.

Jimmie Lee's response was completely reactive; his body immediately leaped into action, protecting him in the ways described earlier in this chapter. Dr. Mosharrafa, however, focused his efforts consciously, applying his intelligence, life experience and medical training in the service of someone in dire need. He acted with pro-urgency.

For Jimmie Lee, the accident was obviously a cause of extreme distress. Dr. Mosharrafa responded in a state of eustress. The situation, though bizarre, was a positive professional and personal challenge for him. Both doctor and patient played their parts in this dramatic life-or-death situation. Reactive urgency met proactive urgency.

Today, Jimmie Lee is an adult in good health, still living in Kentucky. He drives by the tobacco curing barn every day, the scene of the now surreal accident, and is reminded of the fragile nature of life.

Dr. Mosharrafa is a highly respected plastic surgeon in Phoenix, Arizona. He was part of a medical mission to Haiti immediately after the 2010 earthquake. While there, he treated over a hundred people with a wide variety of traumatic injuries—none like Jimmie Lee's. In dealing with traumatic injuries, he is the epitome of pro-urgent action.

First Responders.

Many doctors, police officers, firefighters, emergency room staff and intensive care nurses have chosen professions where their roles as first responders require confrontation with people in states of acute, energetic, *reactive* urgency. Such situations are complicated at best and often dangerous for all involved. In order to be effective in their work, first responders must train extensively to act as calmly and purposefully as possible to achieve their objectives. In their case, pro-urgency stands for both proactive and professional urgency.

Consider the following statement from an FBI guide to violent encounters directed at first responders:

> It is extremely difficult to control one's biological, psychological, and emotional reactions to life and death circumstances. But it is even more difficult to do so without adequate, realistic, and prior training—along with proper mental and physical preparation. Training often determines which persons survive and which ones suffer injury or death. Training that is realistic, repetitive, understandable, and believable, potentially reduces the non-adaptive effects of evolution. In preparing for a highly-charged emotional event, effective and realistic training can reduce its intensity (levels of arousal), *allowing higher cognitive functioning to prevail.*[8]

Choosing Urgency.

A sense of urgency can be proactively created. It can be practiced and perfected. Dr. Mosharrafa and other first responders are proof of this as, for that matter, are Philippe Petit and countless others.

With practice, and in the pursuit of an objective that is sufficiently important, we can to a significant degree create a sense of urgency similar to the kind that drives us when we are confronted with a fight-or-flight situation. However, this kind of *proactive urgency* is, as the term implies, planned, controlled and focused.

Pro-urgency is by definition *not* automatic or reactive. It is purposefully selected as a way of being in the relentless pursuit of a goal you will not be denied. It is manifested in your calculated actions and is engaged with a high level of sustained intensity.

You have probably said it yourself: "I am great in a crisis." If this is true, why wait for a crisis to bring forth the best in you? Why not choose proactive urgency as your *first* choice in the pursuit of something you really care about, rather than waiting for a crisis to induce reactive urgency to force you into giving your best?

You have the choice of being proactively urgent in the service of what matters most to you.

Urgency Rule #2

It is your choice to act with "first responder" urgency outside of an emergency or a crisis. Pro-urgency is a powerful way to engage your highest and best resources to get what you want.

3

The *Sense* in Urgency

There is a palpable difference between an urgent and non-urgent state of mind. We are all familiar with the latter; many of us spend much of our time in less focused, neutral or low-energy states. But urgency-by-choice is the province of the active, directed and decisive mind. This is why the word *urgency* is often used in combination with the word *sense*. The resulting phrase, *sense of urgency*, is much more than an abstract reference.

If you could see and hear me while I attempted to convey to you the need for urgency, you would immediately understand my meaning. Through my emphatic facial expressions, body language and voice amplitude and inflection, you would likely *feel it* too.

Pro-urgency represents a commitment to a higher degree of awareness and engagement than usual. It is not, however, a panacea; it can't and shouldn't be applied with equivalent energy to every aspect of your life. Leave it out of the equation for grocery shopping or getting your teeth cleaned, for example.

But in those situations where you have determined to accept no outcome other than the achievement of a game-changing objective, the application of pro-urgency provides an absolute advantage.

Just Going Faster?

When I first began thinking about the value of urgency engaged in a non-reactive way, my ideas centered on *rapidity*. Most of us have accessed the advantage of speed when doing something we considered important.

It didn't take me long to conclude that the word "rapid" is frequently misapplied. It has become a form of marketing bait to attract people with unrealistic expectations and money to spend. "Rapid" is often an absurdly inappropriate adjective. Is it true, for example, that "rapid weight loss," "rapid psychotherapy" and "rapid transit" accurately describe the time it will take to get to the promised outcome?

In many cases it represents nothing more than wishful thinking. Even worse, speeding up a process that is flawed will simply deliver the same poor results—only faster. "I know how to fix our rapid transit system. Let's run the buses faster and make fewer stops!"

Not useful.

In my experience, when one chooses proactive urgency as a way of proceeding, an appropriate rate of speed will be discovered.

Just Managing Time?

Urgency and *importance* are often spoken about together.

A frequently-cited example of this combination is from the work of Dr. Stephen Covey, including *The 7 Habits of Highly Effective People* and *First Things First*. What follows is a brief reference. If you are interested in more relating to *The 7 Habits*, there is a lot of direct as well as interpretive material available.9

Dr. Covey presents a simple matrix of events and activities. Here is an example (updated for today):

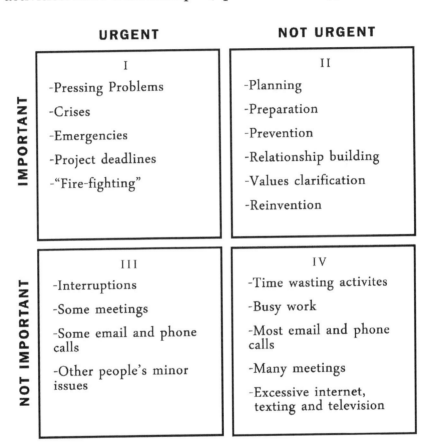

The Covey Matrix

Covey's principal recommendation is that most people spend their time on things in Quadrant II: Important, Not Urgent. The examples offered include activities that involve readiness-making, values and relationships. Being proactive is required, but no passionate edge is called for. In fact, if you read the terms aloud, you almost get a feeling that these things might be best done in a relaxed manner over time.

In the Covey matrix, Quadrant I (Important, Urgent) is concerned with instances in which individuals are pushed or pulled into timely responsiveness by external circumstances. Doesn't this correspond to pro-urgency?

Not quite.

In the examples offered for Quadrant 1, you are required to bring your energy to bear on something that has declared *itself* a priority. Such a pressing problem *might* change your game for the better. But it might just be something demanding to be defused.

A Quadrant I crisis might have to do with paying the bills this month, which, although important at the moment, is certainly not a significant call to transformational action. Beyond the temporary pain relief of having "paid" stamped on your bills, it is not the high-leverage something that is worthy of your all-out effort over time.

As to Quadrants III and IV, Dr. Covey points out that we are ready at an instant to react to or apply ourselves to the routine and mundane. We permit—and by default often invite—clock time to run all over us.

You will recognize these low productivity activities as the ones sucking large amounts of time and attention from your days, weeks and months—at work and at home. Because of our perceived need to deal with this stuff, we often permit it to masquerade as our first priority. Applying our attention to these kinds of tasks and activities enables us to at least *appear* to be both busy and worried.

In our culture we often equate the perception of being anxious (and sometimes the actual time clocked in at the office) with doing something important. In work and other settings, if our brows are furrowed and we seem unduly focused, we are making clear that we are once again engaged in dealing with our crisis *du jour*. We also often feel the need to do our best to look uninterruptable. This can occur even when we are dedicating time and attention to planning things we already know are largely irrelevant and which may never even come to pass.

By way of justifying our active presence in the situation, we ask, "If I don't take care of this, who will?" Eric Hoffer put it this way: "We are more ready to try the untried when what we do is inconsequential."[10] When you see people boldly dealing with trivial undertakings, you will likely never see them addressing things that are *actually* important.

Why is it that we are ready to open ourselves to countless "have you got a minute's?" and a never-ending stream of inane and insignificant interruptions? We willingly occupy ourselves with a random daily bag of text, social media and email messages, nonsensical and irrelevant photos, videos, chats and updates. We simply *must* stay in touch or risk receiving less of all of that important stuff. Or worse, being "defriended"[11] or left out altogether.

You don't need to put any of this numbing white noise into a matrix to know you are spending some fair portion of your life on... *not much at all.*

Urgency-by-choice takes the concept of time management to a different level. You will find that the effort and commitment put into work you have chosen to treat with urgency has nothing to do with clock time. Acting with proactive urgency is about your commitment to the objective, the attentiveness and depth of your focus, the velocity and timeliness of your actions, the fierceness of your pursuit.

If forced to incorporate activities driven by applied urgency into the Covey matrix, I suggest they would represent a superset of Quadrant I. These are not actions taken as a *response* to external circumstances suggesting the need for an immediate reaction. Instead, they are actions you *decide* to take toward an objective that is important enough for you to purposefully pursue with self-generated urgency until you achieve it. Time management becomes a by-product of your urgency.

Go Big.

By definition, engaging in pro-urgency in pursuit of your most important objectives relegates deferral, rationalization and procrastination to diminishing images in your rear view mirror.

As mentioned earlier, not all priorities—even important ones—can be the object of your proactively urgent pursuits. Acting with pro-urgency should be reserved for driving the achievement of significant objectives in your life. Use it as a way of raising your game to a higher level of value creation.

In a business context, Vinod Kholsa, co-founder of Sun Microsystems and a superbly successful Silicon Valley venture capitalist, boiled the risk-reward equation down to its essence. "Any big problem is a big opportunity. No problems, no solutions, no company. It's very simple... If you don't have a big problem, you don't have a big opportunity. Nobody will pay you to solve a non-problem."[12]

He advised welcoming big challenges, valuing them and solving them. In business and in life in general, the pursuit of anything with pro-urgency requires "going big."[†]

What is the Downside?

There is typically no greater risk in moving *with* urgency than there is in moving without it, if appropriate checks and balances are a part of the process.[‡]

Any potential risk in taking thoughtful, urgent action is almost always overstated. Unfortunately, this fact often doesn't become clear until after an opportunity has evaporated.

Most of us have personal histories replete with moments when we chose not to take risks. More often than not we "saved" ourselves not from missteps or failure, but from greater opportunities and success.

Urgency Rule #3

Urgency-by-choice is the province of the active, directed and decisive mind. Your engagement of proactive urgency will be evident from the level of your commitment to the objective, the attentiveness and depth of your focus, the velocity and timeliness of your actions, the fierceness of your pursuit. Engage it in the service of objectives that will be game-changing in your work and your life.

[†] See Chapter 7: *The Pro-Urgent Business.*
[‡] See Chapter 14: *Ongoing Inquiry—What Has Changed?*

4

<u>Self-Reliance – Now More Than Ever</u>

The traditional societal pillars of strength—family and community, work, education and religion, among others— have mostly destabilized, deteriorated or disintegrated over the past fifty years. These pillars once formed essential components of our societal infrastructure. They represented places of safety from which to launch ourselves into the world, to take action, to learn, to discover—and to retreat to when dealing with the pain and isolation we all encounter at one time or another throughout our lives.

What impact have these shifts had on the importance of self-reliance manifested in your engagement with proactive urgency? Before answering that, let's take a look at some of these pillars so that we can better consider the silver lining that I believe is part of the answer to this question.

Family.

The family as the central support system for a small group of connected individuals has become a fractured institution. One factor is the decline in family formation that traditionally resulted from marriage. Over the past forty years the marriage rate per thousand of U.S. population has dropped from 10.6 to 6.8.[13]

More importantly, for all too many the family unit often lacks the commitment that was once the glue binding its individual members together. Absent moms and dads have created an opening for online worlds and social networks (for family members of all ages) to displace the traditional family structure.

As soon as small children are no longer small, even they can be seen making arrangements to spend more and more time with their own online and offline social groups. If you think I am wrong, what do you think a smartphone in the hands of a seventh grader represents? Children of all ages loosely band together for support, with retreats to the home base from time-to-time. The virtual world has become the new, much less controlled "village," as in, "it takes a village to raise a child."

On a broader scale this applies to communities as well. Once an extended support system, or at least a positive presence, the community has diminished in its influence, leading to yet another sense of disconnection. In the case of the traditional community made up in part of its residents and businesses, to some significant extent it has been displaced by the online Facebook Nation (and many other internet options).

We are a people on the move. Many roots and commitments that were once deep have become shallow and more readily and willingly transplanted. When this happens, the family—once life's central support system for many people—gives way to a mixed bag of outside influences with a wide range of objectives and tactics to get what they want.

Work.

Work and employment were once a central linkage with our parents, families, neighbors and communities. People often worked for their entire careers with one company and then retired with the thanks and ongoing support of the employer. The gold watch may have been more symbolic than an object of great value, but it defined the conclusion of an important relationship for the company and the person involved, as well as for the broader community.[14]

This perhaps somewhat idealized relationship has, based upon economics and global competition, given way to the decline of cohesive labor organizations, fractionalization of work, and transient employer and employee populations— often with competition, if not outright bitterness, between them.

Non-retirement has now also come into view and changed the workplace mix and dynamics for all ages. People must work well beyond the traditional age of retirement in order to sustain themselves through their so-called golden years. The workplace will never be the same (wherever the workplace may be found in an ever more virtual world).

Education.

It was once believed that acquiring an education was essential in order to enter the workforce at a higher level and be an informed citizen capable of contributing to the greater good.

The cost for in-state tuition at a four-year public college has risen by 104% over the past ten years.[15] Over the same period, the lifetime economic value of that investment of money and time has come into question. Fewer and fewer aspiring students want to be troubled by going through the higher education process (and in many cases the associated accumulation of debt) only to face the now significant prospect of unemployment upon graduation. Not going to college removes yet another societal platform from which to go forth and conquer with the support of a community of interests (faculty, fellow students and the institution itself).

The ubiquity and breakaway success of online learning is causing the physical facilities in the form of traditional campuses to be less relevant. The new campuses are virtual worlds with opportunities for interaction with program managers (formerly called "faculty") and students through social media specific to the program. It is not just technology that is driving this educational morphology. This model is efficient, lean, and convenient, and produces a high level of cash flow and potential profitability for the campus "operator."

I suspect that many physical campuses will ultimately disappear altogether. As that occurs, the traditional four-year opportunity for socialization, personal growth and maturity—an important rite of passage for many young people entering the adult world—will vanish as well.

Religion.

Traditional religious institutions as a central societal foundation have for some time been giving way to secularization and seeking in many flavors.[16] In addition to wholesale departures from the major religions, we see a growing number of humanists, atheists, agnostics, secularists and free thinkers. A recent Pew Research Center poll revealed that "nones"—those who say they have no religious affiliation at all—now account for 20% of the U.S. population, up from 16% in 2008.[17]

The Gallup Organization found in a survey published in 2012 that "Forty-four percent of Americans have a great deal or quite a lot of confidence in "the church or organized religion." This is the lowest point Gallup has found in recent years and represents a slide from earlier highs of almost 70% in the mid 1970s.[18]

In a *New York Times* opinion piece written by Molly Worthen, she opined, "The temple of 'my personal opinion' may be the real 'established church' in modern America . . . Americans are drifting out of the grip of institutionalized religion, just as they are drifting from institutional authority in general."[19] The roof isn't falling in on it, but religion as one of the major pillars we once relied upon is giving way to a variety of competing interests and alternatives.

The Upside of Risk.

With the weakening of institutions that once provided structure and a measure of perceived safety, the importance of individual self-reliance is clear. The power and differentiation inherent in acting with urgency-by-choice becomes even more meaningful with a self-reliant mindset.

In times of upheaval both losers and winners find new points of equilibrium. Today an increasing level of dynamic complexity exists in the areas of information processing, communication, competition and innovation—essentially *everywhere*. This has created a super-premium opportunity for anyone who can engage in rapid assessment, prioritization, decision making and timely adjustments based on real-world feedback.

In short, for anyone acting with proactive urgency as a manifestation of a new form of *very purposeful* self-reliance.

Consider self-reliance your mandate whether in your work as an entrepreneur, as a brave agent of change toiling in a larger organization, or simply as an individual aspiring to be the best you can be as a human being.

According to PwC's chairman and senior partner, Robert E. Moritz, changes in the speed and connectedness of our world have us living and working in an environment that possesses a higher element of risk as a constant state rather than an exception. In an interview with the HBR Blog Network, he comments, "The world has absolutely become more uncertain—and in more ways. First, you have a great many uncertain political and economic events, as well as a highly uncertain regulatory environment. Second, new communication vehicles have radically increased transparency. And third, we have instantaneous movement of data, actions, and points of view. The combination of these three has created what I'd call a new world order of risk."[20]

I would suggest that these risk elements have an equal if not greater measure of *opportunity* associated with them.§

Self-Reliance.

The time is now to understand that the answers required for a fulfilling life are not outside of you. Although the societal supports I referenced above have value individually and collectively, given the speed of change and the impermanence factor they cannot be counted upon for many of the answers we may require. Acting with pro-urgency has always had value, but this is true now more than ever.

---

§ More about this relating to business opportunities in Chapter 7: *The Pro-Urgent Business.*

The outside is always pulling and begging and insisting that the answers are there. They aren't. The answers for an authentic, challenging, rewarding and energizing life are already contained in who you are today.

Every person's DNA is different from all other humans and all other life forms. Each of us is truly one-of-a-kind. Engaging your uniqueness in the drive for your highest purposes can take you as far as you are willing to extend yourself.

Supercharge your approach in your own best interests. Choose to pursue the most important objectives in your life by engaging your own unique brand of proactive urgency.

If you are 20, 32, 53 or even 74, you needn't wait for greater wisdom to arrive on some undefined future date. You need only access the knowledge, strength, power and uniqueness you already possess.

Simply put, if you care about creating a self-reliant life you have no choice other than embracing proactive, applied urgency in seeking to achieve your most important goals— starting now.

Urgency Rule #4

The world has changed. Our long-trusted external support systems are weakening. Self-reliance in thought and action is critical for reaching your most important objectives.

5

Discovering Personal Urgency

I often work as an agent of change—a catalyst for action—serving people in and outside of businesses for whom the status quo will no longer be tolerated. I didn't start out with this as my calling. As my life has unfolded, my education, work and relationship experiences, along with my ability to engage with the right attitude, have made this my urgently pursued mission in life. And, as is often the case when you are led in a specific direction, aptitude seems to go along with it. Or maybe it's a chicken and egg situation. It doesn't really matter.

It so happens that I love being in the vortex of creating urgency with others or teaching people and organizations how to shift from the status quo to a state of active engagement.

Occasionally I am contacted about my work and hear, "Things are going pretty well now, but we can see how this might turn into a situation we won't be able to tolerate if enough time goes by and our results decline." This kind of admirable anticipation calls for developing options that can be deployed when the need arises. A pro-urgent strategy in such situations can certainly prove effective—though it may not generate the same degree of intensity for those involved as it does when circumstances are more pressing.

Far more frequently I receive calls indicating that the status quo is well on its way to becoming the "status rigor mortis," or close to it. This sometimes presents itself as a real crisis with a ticking time bomb attached to it.

The nature of most human beings (including business managers) is to be slow to realize that a situation is degrading until it has real consequences. In other words clarity arrives suddenly, when the situation has reached the point where it requires immediate triage and reformation into something better, with no more waiting.

Opening the Connection.

One of my favorite starter questions for opening a conversation with a client is "How did you come to be here?"

For an individual, an answer can begin at the beginning: "I was born during a blizzard..." Or it can be literal, as in, "I took the 101 South to the 202 East and exited onto Central Avenue." Or it could go much deeper: "My wife and I are going to outlive our money and we can't keep up appearances any longer..."

For a business, the answer might be: "The go-to-market approach that worked for us over the past seventeen years has become a competitive disadvantage." Or, "In order to survive, we have to expand outside the U.S., and we have no idea how or where to begin." Or it could be clearer cut (with the proverbial ticking time bomb attached): "My investors have given me three months to create a positive shift in the financial performance of the company..."

The question is simple—and the answer can reveal much—but whatever comes forth represents my entry point into their world. This is where insight begins and where the mutual trust that will enable powerful interaction is born. This is the starting point for a pro-urgent effort.

The question, "How did I come to be here?" is also a good one to ask yourself from time-to-time.

The answers that come up for you offer the opportunity to review your personal inventory of experiences, education, interests, values and character. You may discover or rediscover special skills, attributes or capabilities that can provide unique leverage to engage in your own service and in that of others.

The answers that come up in a business context offer the same opportunity for a reassessment of the current state of things, and for a new look at what is possible in terms of the choices available for action.

When I embraced my current incarnation—trusted advisor, change agent, author, speaker—I took stock of what made up the unique "me" that I am. I reviewed my skills and experience to clearly define my assets and resources. My ability to assess complex situations and challenges and to get into action with a sense of urgency rose to the top of the list.

Ultimately I recognized within myself an ability to make my best assets work for those I serve, and for me. It also became clear that I could articulate the key elements, attitudes and process for "what to do" for the benefit of others—this book is one result. All of these realizations flowed from the inquiry "How did I come to be here?"

School Days Here and There.

I believe I was blessed with DNA containing the foundational elements for engaging in rapid assessment, prioritization and action. But added to this were the education, experiences and learning opportunities I had growing up and as an adult.

When I was a kid, I lived in eight different places over the course of sixteen years of primary, middle and high school. On average, we moved every other year. On a number of occasions it was several years before we would land in one place for any length of time.

I wasn't conscious of it then, but this life-in-motion would end up defining me in almost every way.

I can illustrate this by sharing something that happened when I was going into fifth grade. We had recently moved from a small Illinois farming town of five hundred people to Chicago, one of the biggest cities in the country. We moved from a house to an apartment. I was transplanted from a small school where I knew everyone to one so big it was impossible to know all the kids just in my grade.

But by then I had experience coping with this kind of change. I knew I couldn't wait long to make friends or get involved in activities as a way of staking out ground in the new scene. I knew if I didn't start immediately I would remain an outsider—the new kid—for the rest of the time I was there. Until our inevitable next move.

As an introvert, more-or-less, this desire to find a spot in a new environment required that I overcome the discomfort I felt in new places, around new people and in new situations. I learned how to quickly and accurately assess the existing hierarchies and to position myself on the margin of several groups (but not in the center of any). I observed and absorbed information, then integrated it as I saw fit based on what I sensed—not necessarily what I knew.

Midway through the school year I had another opportunity to test my developing skills. Although I was among the youngest in my current class, I was selected for mid-year promotion to the next grade. I didn't know a single person in the new class. The first half of the course material was already completed and it was not at all clear to me how I would manage to make the two-grades-in-one-year program work.

But, like being forced to fly after falling out of the nest, I quickly adapted to the situation by assessing the environment and finding my place in it. It was impossible to do anything but be academically behind everyone else for the rest of the year, but I nonetheless could make friends and enjoy my remaining time. Once I figured that out, I was able to accept that "this is where I am" for three months before we returned to the town we had left less than a year before.

I wasn't yet ten years old.

I didn't realize at the time that I was learning coping skills broadly applicable to higher-order problem solving. I was simply working to overcome the "new kid" label and fit in. It turned out that going through this process over and over was a step in the direction of becoming a master change agent.

Much Seeking, Ultimately Finding.

My development as a future change creator, catalyst and manager continued throughout my teen years and into adulthood. I became an active seeker of new places, homes, people, careers, experiences and interests. I became further adept at rapidly sizing up new situations and quickly charting a course toward mastery of the new environment.

It would be nice to say that I did all this gracefully and by design. I didn't. You can probably guess that my life was full of disruption, unnecessary moves and abandonment of perfectly good—in some cases outstanding—work and personal relationships. I left a fair amount of not-so-great flotsam and jetsam bobbing in my wake.

But now I can say that change for the sake of change is, thankfully, off the table for me.

Though I didn't realize it until much later, the way I coped with personal challenges and mastered my ever-changing environments along the way became central to the development of my unique way of pursuing achievement that I share with you in these pages as proactive urgency.

It turned out that what I thought were merely unfortunate childhood and adult experiences served as the foundation for the development of a powerful way of approaching life and its challenges. Accepting and overcoming those challenges ultimately enabled me to develop the skill of assessing, prioritizing and taking urgent action—all in one motion—and sustaining it for as long as necessary. Understanding this process and how to share it with others led to my stock-in-trade as a leader, change agent and guide for business and personal transformation pursued with a committed and urgent state of mind.

My understanding of these strengths came from an "aha"—or perhaps better expressed as a "duh"—moment, after examining the experiences I once viewed as negative and completely irrelevant to the big picture. It took a look through the "other end of the telescope." It was about seeing challenges that may at the time have been overwhelming as also containing the seeds of defining strengths developed through necessity.

Consider in your own circumstances how the experience of getting over difficult hurdles may have provided you with more personal firepower than you recognized at the time. What untapped tools and resources can you discover in your individual "inventory" that you might have put aside because they arose from experiences that were painful or negative at the time?

Could those experiences be reframed to provide you with new insights and personal power today?

This was certainly true in my case. Today these now-polished assets form a good part of the centerpiece of my service to others.

What Will Go in the Dumpster?

Along with evaluating your experiences to find hidden skills and strengths, it can also help to create your life today with a greater awareness of the realities and possibilities of the future. In my case, I have found extraordinary value and personal power in living each day consciously aware of my inevitable mortality. For me, that awareness is a continuous reminder of the value of each moment and the need to remain crystal clear about what is important and what is irrelevant *for me.*

For some, this practice might seem morbid or gloomy rather than empowering. But this awareness can in and of itself be a motivating force. It can be a point of leverage for more powerful daily living. If you simply consider the likely number of days remaining in your life, that knowledge can help guide your choices and your level of urgency.[21] It is not about focusing on the "end." It is about squeezing all of the juice from life while we have the opportunity.

I feel so strongly about opening to a full appreciation of our limited lifespans that I wrote an award-winning book about it entitled, *LIFE Expectancy: It's Never Too Late to Change Your Game.*[22] The essence of its message is that no matter where you are in life or how accomplished you are—or are not—understanding your mortality in personal as opposed to abstract terms can be a terrific motivator to get moving and keep moving.

No waiting. No rationalizing. No whining. Just pure, purposeful action infused with all the urgency-by-design you can muster.

You might connect with a word picture that resonated loudly with me. Jonathan Fields is an author, blogger and observer who writes about work, life, play and entrepreneurship.[23]

He wrote a short blog entitled "Dust in the Wind?" Here it is:

> There are a lot of elderly folks, many of them widows and widowers, who live in my building. Every winter, a parade of dumpsters end up alongside the building. Vessels that port away the contents of the homes of those who've passed. My apartment looks down on the spot where the dumpsters get dropped. The image you are looking at replaces itself on a regular basis. Precious items, keepsakes, valuable mementos, furniture, marvelous art—all sent to a landfill. This is what's left of someone's life. Not the experiences, but the stuff.[24]

Could knowing that all your stuff (even the *good* stuff) might end up in a dumpster change anything about what you plan to do with yourself for the rest of your day, week or life?

Each to their own interpretation of course. But consider that all you really have of lasting value are your experiences and memories. Experiences—and the time they take—are priceless.

You can fit a lot more life than you think into the time you are blessed to have. Acting with pro-urgency can help you do it. Ultimately, the stuff you leave behind won't matter to you anyway.

© Charles McNally

Experiences aren't welcome here.

Urgency Rule #5

Take an inventory of your personal strengths and weaknesses. You will find that in apparent weakness lies amazing personal power. Permit the awareness of the finite nature of your life to fuel your personal urgency.

6

<u>A 1% Advantage</u>

When our efforts are infused with urgency they are significantly more focused and powerful.

We all know how acting with urgency feels when we are doing it.

Can this feeling be created at will?

If you have ever purposefully created a crisis of any kind, you know the answer. Most of us have, at the very least, established artificial deadlines for ourselves or others as a way of increasing the pressure to complete the task at hand. This is a form of creating urgency through the use of limitation.

Even without a crisis we have the ability to create with proactive urgency—and engage the requisite passionate edge—anytime we choose. It is far more than merely a random sense of directed power that shows up on its own.

It can be created.

It can be developed.

It can be practiced.

It can be replicated.

Pro-urgency can be used to drive the actions necessary for our most desired outcomes.

Wins By Fractions.

Can the personal power generated through acting with urgency-by-choice enable us to reach the levels of performance possible in a confrontation with a life-or-death situation? In short, can pro-urgency be as intense as crisis- or emergency-based reactive urgency?

The answer is an emphatic "No."

But what if through your actions with proactive urgency you could capture 80% of the energy and focus available in a fight-or-flight context? What about 50%? What do you think you need in the way of incremental energy and focus to more consistently achieve your most important objectives?

If being proactively urgent could consistently ensure even a *1% advantage*, would it be worth it?

Being 1% faster than the rest of the sprinters in a highly competitive hundred-meter race is typically more than sufficient to win. Winning a basketball game by one point is as good as winning by fifty. The same is true for the one point difference between an A and a B on a test, and winning an election by a single vote.

Winning by a fraction is still winning.

I believe that acting with purposeful urgency will typically deliver incremental advantages *much greater* than 1%. The more you use it, and the greater the edge you bring to it, the bigger the gains available. This kind of advantage can consistently be yours by choosing to lead and create with the power of urgency.

Hurry-Up.

Most of us have heard of the football term known as the "hurry-up offense."

Professional football teams often shift into this style of play in late-game situations. It is also sometimes called the "two-minute drill." "Hurry-up" typically refers to an increased sense of urgency being engaged by the team that is behind. It can also be used by the team in the lead in order to sustain or improve its advantage.

The result, if all goes according to plan, is running more plays than the team would normally run in the same allotment of time. Football teams at all levels have taken to using this kind of speeded-up offense at earlier points in the game, when there is a need or desire to shift or extend the momentum.

In terms of the overarching strategies of the game, the offense is typically considered to have the advantage. This is simply because the offensive players know in advance what play is coming next and the defensive players don't. In order to minimize that advantage, the players on defense have to rely on their knowledge of the tendencies of the offensive team and continue to make modifications as the game unfolds. Often you will hear a sideline reporter ask the coach whose team is behind at halftime, "What adjustments will you make for the second half?"

A football team that plays the hurry-up style of offense doubles its advantage.

Not only does the offense have the advantage of knowing the next play, they place even more pressure on the defense by speeding up the game. Another bonus for the offense is that the conditioning of the defense will be severely tested if a drive continues down the field without the offense spending significant time on huddles. After a while you might hear the defensive players being described as "gassed." This is because their recovery period between plays is drastically reduced when the offense huddles only briefly—or not at all.

Some college coaches have made the hurry-up offense their particular brand of football and run it frequently. These coaches have chosen the path of proactive urgency for their teams.

One of those teams is at Baylor University. Its head coach, Art Briles, has been an important offensive innovator of the game for the past twenty years. Some consider him to be the godfather of the speed game of college football.

My college alma mater, Eastern Illinois University, hired Dino Babers, then a senior assistant on Coach Briles' staff, to be its head football coach. At the time he was hired, the EIU program had been underperforming, and in the previous season the team had finished last in its conference.

We Choose to Work with What We Have.

Coach Babers had the opportunity to create a new incarnation of the EIU football team. But because of the timing of his hire, he had to work with the players that were already there. Those athletes for the most part had not been recruited because of their exceptional speed, quickness or conditioning. But Babers had to work with the hand he was dealt; he couldn't—and wouldn't—wait for the proverbial next year.

The time was now.

He accepted the football resources that he had inherited and made clear his intention for the Panthers' offense to be more impactful and interesting from a spectator point of view—and, of course, to win more games.

Based upon his experience with Coach Briles he firmly believed that this type of commitment required going far deeper than merely playing faster football. His intention was that everyone associated with the team—coaches, players, support staff and administration—would address their responsibilities with great commitment and consistent urgency.

When I asked Coach Babers to explain his approach, he said, "The practice routine we live by is aligned with how we play on game days. When we line up for the play we do it urgently. When we finish the play we do everything we can to move to the next play as quickly as is possible. When we rest, we do it completely. We get every bit of value out of our resting time by being completely still and quiet."[25]

He went on to say, "Our kids are excited about this and they bring all of their own life experiences to bear to help build this program to win by playing a hurry-up style."

This is a great example of creating a sense of urgency within an organization by training each of the team members to execute their part of the plan in a way that collectively keeps the pressure on the competition. In this case, the preparation includes better conditioning, a deeper level of commitment, sometimes going faster than feels comfortable and seeing risk as carrying the potential for gain and not as something to be avoided.

It also requires an appreciation of the fact that the entire *team* organization must operate with collective pro-urgency, rather than just the coaches and a few highly-skilled players. This is true for every type of team, from football to a business organization.

Eastern Illinois University

Coach Dino Babers

Measuring Success.

Nobody expected things to change overnight, but they did.

In Coach Babers' first year at the helm, EIU posted a 6-1 record in the Ohio Valley Conference and won the regular season championship. The previous year they had finished last. They finished the season with a national rank of twenty-five in both the final Sports Network poll and the FCS Coaches poll. The team ranked among the nation's top-ten FCS programs in scoring offense, passing offense and total offense. The previous year they couldn't be found near the top ten.

Coach Babers was voted the conference's Football Coach of the Year and finished third in voting for college football's national Eddie Robinson Award.

In one year, through his leadership, passion and commitment, Babers had created a form of repeatable urgency—sustainable in a succession of short bursts.

This is the power of applied urgency in action.

It isn't randomness or luck or fate at work.

It is *preparation* meeting *opportunity*.

Every one of us can do it.

Urgency Rule #6

Choosing to act with on-demand urgency yields continuous, incremental advantages. Think of pro-urgency as your edge in a competition—*your life*—where winning by fractions always matters.

7

The Pro-Urgent Business

Pro-urgency can be utilized in directing the strategies and operations of enterprises of all sizes. Much of what I synthesize here about acting with proactive urgency is a result of my work with businesses as an entrepreneur, executive, board member, investor and trusted advisor.

I have personally witnessed business leaders and managers embrace urgency as an imperative and improve their strategies, fundamentals and financial performance faster than they ever thought possible. Embracing the power of urgency is an effective way to position your business not simply to survive, but to thrive.

The Road to Hell.

The roadside is littered with the carcasses of companies and other institutions that relied upon a belief that whatever strategy, business model, product, service or expanding market that worked to get them into the fast lane would suffice to keep them there. What is often the case in such situations is that management ultimately permits what they "know"—that is, what has worked in the past—to get in the way of what is necessary and possible with an ongoing commitment to transformation.

Chris Zook, co-head of the Global Strategy Practice at Bain & Company, writes:

"We are clearly entering a period where the extinction of the slow, the inflexible, and the bureaucratic is about to happen in record numbers. [We] have been tracking this for forty years, and we have never seen companies losing their leadership positions as quickly as they are today. . . [We] have come to the conclusion that the extinction of once-great innovators is less often caused by technological or market evolution, and more often by self-inflicted wounds and slow cycles of decision and adaptation."[26]

He is describing the *absence* of engagement with pro-urgency in pursuit of the most important objectives, issues, and challenges facing a business.

Most of us have heard some variation on the following: "We have done it this way for thirty-seven years. Everyone's comfortable with it. It would be risky to change or move too quickly."

Ask Montgomery Ward, Polaroid, Borders, Blockbuster or Hostess about the wisdom of this as a "strategy." Ask most of the previously dominant players in the print newspaper industry. Better yet, ask their former shareholders, employees and other constituents.

In another context, ask Penn State about the damage done through the "going along" culture that culminated in the Sandusky scandal. Better yet, ask the Penn State students, academic faculty, alumnae and donors, and the merchants and citizens of State College, Pennsylvania.

There is a certain arrogance in hanging onto a methodical, slow-moving, low-vision and protectionist management approach when the circumstances have changed and the pace has accelerated for all to see.

C.S. Lewis said, "The safest road to hell is the gradual one—the gentle slope, soft underfoot, without sudden turnings, without milestones, without signposts." Could the course of events have been different in any of the cases cited above? Could the forced transformations, serious damage to or complete failure of these businesses and institutions have been avoided?

We can relate the benefits of purposefully acting with urgency to the approaches of the best competitors in the marketplace. If competitors are equal in every other way, executing key elements of your business with a higher degree of urgency can both assure a market advantage and keep you off the road to hell.

Look around your community, business sector and industry; read any business magazine, newspaper or other publication in the U.S or anywhere in the world; take a look at what underpins the companies recognized for best practices. You will see—and if you could get close enough, you would *feel*—the *passionate edge* of urgency as a part of a high-performing business and culture.

There is no sugar-coating the reality and it isn't a secret. If you want your business to survive *and* have a shot at thriving year-in and year-out, you have no option but to integrate pro-urgency into your management approach for the things that really count.

Pro-Urgent Management.

Quality in the decision-making process has always been a differentiator for achieving business success. Speed, flexibility and adaptability in making decisions has now become as significant a competitive advantage as management, capital, marketing or any other factor you care to name. The attributes of speed, flexibility and adaptability in business are sometimes collectively referred to as business "agility."

Agility for a business, and a sense of urgency for that matter, is first and foremost a consequence of individual commitment and leadership. It results when leadership sets the tone for acting with a greater sense of urgency and enough individuals subscribe to—and act upon—a course of agile decision making and adaptation to the point where it becomes a cultural imperative.

In the small and medium-sized organizations making up the huge numbers of the bottom sections of the pyramid of all businesses, this kind of change is much closer to hand-to-hand combat than it is to carpet bombing. It is *very* personal, and typically depends upon a few committed individuals, perhaps founders, owner-operators, board members, investors and trusted advisors.

Some are better equipped for rapid adaptation than others. In fact, nearly half of executives surveyed globally by the consulting firm Accenture ". . . have little confidence in their companies' ability to mobilize quickly to capitalize on market shifts or to serve new customers. Half do not believe that their culture is adaptive enough to respond positively to change . . . They also view volatility as a limitation rather than an opportunity."[27]

This Accenture report focuses on the topic of corporate agility and ways to create a shift in the direction of it. It includes a twelve-point agility checklist. The questions contained in it have value not only for leaders and managers in businesses of all sizes, but for individuals embarking on the road to selected achievement with pro-urgency. I have included the list in its entirety in the endnotes.[28]

One of the great challenges for a business needing rejuvenation or reinvention is to suspend belief about what worked in the past—but which is no longer working today— long enough either to enable the creation of something new or to reconstitute the status quo in creative and transformative ways. Embracing the concepts of pro-urgency and agility as imperative for businesses of all sizes makes it possible to anticipate and create transformation—rather than racing to catch up with a seemingly sudden requirement for it through after-the-fact reactions.

Choosing proactive urgency as a modus operandi is a commitment to agility and rapid adaptation.

Why Wait?

Humans are equipped to remember, access and put into context more information than they even know they possess.** A starting point for introducing the process of pro-urgency to the employees in your business is to make clear that they have permission to move quickly toward a solution based upon what they already know, as opposed to what they have yet to discover or "analyze."

By simply offering this minor freedom—shifting focus from *completion* of the process to the deeper solution *driving* the process—you will see amazing results. You will also see energized people making decisions without days or weeks or months passing—and not deferring action until just the *right* piece of information arrives.

** See Chapter 8: *Consciousness—You Know What You Need to Know.*

In life, and in work as a part of it, most of us have been taught that making good choices requires intelligence, analysis, objectivity and the passage of a certain amount of clock time. It is certainly true that these and other factors often play a positive role in good decision making.

But if you knew you could make decisions with an 80% confidence level, and had a greater than 90% opportunity to monitor and adjust those decisions based on feedback received after acting on them, I suspect you would take the bet in almost every case. Not only that, you would feel *great* about it.

Take a look back at how many times a decision made with a confidence level of 80% or so served your business better than getting closer to 100%. In most situations, making a decision with a 100% confidence level is a fantasy anyway (and waiting for one is a form of procrastination, if not insanity). A willingness to pull the trigger at or near the 80% level enables you to *keep moving*. It provides a good (or good enough) point for departure into action and enables moving ahead with sufficient information to feel confident about the choice.

After this, you engage in very timely course corrections as you go—rather than waiting, again, to have the appropriate checklist completed before acting. If you choose the latter option, you could still be sitting in the lobby long after your competition has left the building with the order.

I am not offering my assessment as science here, but in many situations acting with pro-urgency can enable these kinds of confidence levels and opportunities. In my personal and work experience I have found that planning and decision making of all kinds can be done in a fraction of the time typically allotted for it. The same is true for adaptive decisions.

Accomplishing this involves reframing the way you look at the situation. Instead of focusing on what is *missing* from your materials and *lacking* in your process, concentrate your attention on what you *have and know* already. Connect the dots from that base of *knowing* to your *desired outcomes*. And then push forward to get it done in the most efficient way possible.

Challenge yourself about how quickly you can make this happen. Instead of two months, how about two days, or even two *hours*? Take the challenge. It can be done. And remember, once you have achieved acceleration, the opportunity to make course corrections based on updated information is part of the process.

Many owners, executives and board members understand that more agile and iterative decision making could serve the best interests of their business. But when it comes to actually making the decision, cold or slow feet can result in the status quo being maintained. We have all heard some version of "Speeding up decisions and processes in other kinds of businesses may be okay. But trying to do it *here* would be reckless and foolhardy."

As recent history is proving in ever greater numbers, deferral of difficult decisions can mean business suicide. Excessive analysis is procrastination in disguise, and it unfortunately gets a pass in many organizations as a "respectable" excuse for failing to take timely action.

It is also a great cover for fear of pulling the trigger. "We only get one shot, so we have to be sure." Really? What about your competitor with the barrel of a laser-sighted rifle pointed at your forehead? How long until they are "sure" about pulling the trigger? There are very few business environments today where you will find yourself the only competitor with a rifle and at least one bullet.

Make a move in the direction of the kind of *sufficient analysis* that is as responsible and complete and timely as possible under the circumstances. At the same time, embrace a leadership style that enables your employees to act with pro-urgency—at least in the direction of *one* important organizational objective. Do this by enabling decisions to be made with no waiting and coupled with very rapid corrective actions made as soon as they are warranted.

It needn't be an all or nothing proposition. Whenever you see or hear the word *urgency*, recognize the potential to follow your new course in thoughtful, selected, deliberate and risk-adjusted ways. Proactive urgency and intelligent action are far from mutually exclusive.

In fact, the *best* decisions are usually those made in a state of urgency-by-choice, and which are then just as urgently monitored, reviewed and adjusted.[††] If you and your team are "great in a crisis," stay in crisis more often—even if you have to create one on an ongoing basis.

Faster, Cheaper, Better.

There is a well-known rule for the creation of business success and differentiation associated with delivering products and services "faster, cheaper and better."[29]

We all have the capacity to generate great ideas (sometimes even brilliant ones) and at times to engage in outstanding planning and even better execution. We may

---

[††] See Chapter 13: *What Has Changed?*

occasionally be blessed with access to unlimited capital and other resources.

In such a case, embracing and executing *faster* than the other guys can be just the ticket. If you're both doing the same thing, whoever makes "it" happen more urgently will score first and have the "first mover advantage." In many cases, even being a great second mover[30] or fast follower can provide a meaningful advantage. For example, McDonalds followed White Castle and Pampers followed Chux. White Castle and Chux were first in time and became secondary in market awareness and success. If you are asking yourself, "What is Chux?" the point has been illustrated.

The Accenture publication included the statement, ". . . the 'fast follower' tactics that worked before will not work now. In today's tumultuous environment, it is essential to be a fast *leader*."[31] I believe that by infusing your actions with pro-urgency, there is room for first *movers*, fast *followers and* fast *leaders*. The common element is timely and agile leadership coupled with urgent execution.

Why not lead your organization in the inquiry: "Is it possible that making quality decisions is taking longer than it needs to?" As noted above, if your organization is committed to acting with a greater sense of urgency, it can quickly access the more-or-less 80% of the answers you need to move forward. In most cases, you've already got them.

Create a little space for thinking about the potential impact of infusing an element of proactive urgency into your company culture. While you're at it, add some selected *urgent planning* to the equation. You may find that your team relishes the opportunity to shift to a higher gear and step on the accelerator. Along the way you can develop appropriate checks and balances given the risk tolerance your company and its constituents are willing to tolerate.

In today's world, though, you should always be in the process of raising the bar of that tolerance. As you will read in Chapter 11, there is no place to hide. If you are in the game, *you are in the game*—period. Responsible management is about risk awareness and management, not risk avoidance.

No Surprises.

I didn't have to look very far to find a business and a leader I would describe as iconic in terms of winning through the practiced application of pro-urgency.

Wolfgang Koester is founder and CEO of FiREapps, a provider of cloud-based management of foreign currency risks for multinational companies.[32] He is a client of mine.

Here is a quick primer on the problem his company solves.

Currency volatility is a financial risk faced by virtually every multinational company. More than 80% of the revenue of a typical S&P 500 company originates outside its home country. When doing business denominated in foreign currencies, there is significant financial risk because the values of those currencies rise and fall relative to the dollar.

During a recent quarter, 205 public companies reported a $22.7 billion negative revenue impact from currency fluctuations.[33] This is just one proof that if this risk element is left unmanaged, it can have a huge impact on a company's earnings. If it is properly managed, however, the risk can be greatly diminished, in many cases almost to the point of immateriality.

This speaks to what motivated Mr. Koester to develop the solution and bring the company to life. When I discussed FiREapps with him, he said, "I wanted to build this business to solve not only a huge problem, but to create the type of solution about which our team—including me—could have a passionate conviction."

He has a fervent belief in the value of his company's solutions and wants his prospective clients to have the benefit of them. For him, it's less a matter of selling than it is proselytizing.

He believes so strongly in the value of his company's foreign currency risk management solutions that if a prospective client says, "No thank-you," to his asking for their business, he will reply, "I know much more about the value of this solution to your business and financial performance than you do. I am convinced that if you understood what I am offering, you would say yes. So let's continue the conversation and I will do better at making this clear."

It is obvious that he doesn't lack confidence. He knows the real value of his solution to the client's currency risk exposure. He simply believes it is *his* shortcoming that he hasn't yet been able to clearly convey that value to the potential client.

Pro-Urgency's Passionate Edge.

"You don't create urgency by setting goals. You create it by finding ways to have passion for your solution. Your conviction is based on the reality that your solution will absolutely eliminate major pain for the client," observes Koester.

This all starts with him. Mr. Koester is German-born, and he shared this saying with me. *"Erwarte nicht von anderen, was du von dir selbst erwartest."* Don't expect of others more than you expect of yourself.

He knows that if *he* is not convinced of the value of the solutions—and therefore convincing in his conversations with clients—then the rest of the people in his organization cannot be. He knows he must set the proper tone.

He is the most passionate individual in the company about contributing to the success of its clients. He believes he cannot expect others to act with conviction if he does not set the example himself.

"With our clients, only results count, and we usually are called in when a lot of the shareholders' money has already been left on the table in the form of currency losses. We have created processes in our firm that enable us to proactively create powerful solutions for our clients and to consistently deliver."

Shortly after he started the business, two people managed foreign currency risks for six companies. They used spreadsheets and dealt with approximately *100,000* transactions per year.

Today the management is based on complex, dynamic software algorithms developed over the past twelve years. FiREapps solutions are now served up for over 130 companies worldwide. In just a few years the business grew to where it now handles over *three trillion* transactions per year. It is no accident and it is not luck.

"In my business," says Koester, "how we serve our clients is a mirror of our organization. We care about what we do, and we care enough to consistently act with urgency to add value for our clients."

In the early days of building the business, when public companies reported their quarterly results, company executives might deliver along with them words to the effect of "Our base business performed really well, but we got surprised by the impact of the declining value of the Euro versus the dollar. This offset all of our profits for the quarter."

Wolfgang Koester's passion in life is to ensure that his clients never have to say this. His success in this endeavor is attested to by a client retention rate of 97%.

You know enough about pro-urgency to test drive it on an initiative without risking your business. You won't believe what you can accomplish.

Urgency Rule #7

As an organizational leader at any level, commit yourself and your associates to a single important objective to pursue with proactive urgency and a passionate edge—starting now. Your formula for success: 80%-plus confidence-level decisions with continuous monitoring and timely correction.

8

Consciousness – You Know
What You Need to Know

You already know much more than you think you do about urgently pursuing your key objectives. In Chapter 5 I reminded you that each of us possesses experiences, knowledge and perceptions that no one else has. I suggested the question "How did I come to be here?" as a way of beginning to take stock of your personal assets and resources and marshaling them for your advantage.

When you ask this question, much of what you have learned through formal education, personal experience, work history, and many kinds of self-directed inquiries will readily come to mind. Your answers represent conscious resources that are readily available to you.

But you also have a storehouse of less obvious tools. You use them every day, probably without thinking about them or consciously understanding how they work. Whether we realize it or not, all of us regularly draw from resources available at all levels of our beings, not just the ones that are "top-of-the-mind."

Although I believe that acting with proactive urgency is in many respects a highly pragmatic and concrete process, I have come to appreciate that there is more at work in the process than just our brains and other cognitive functions.34 The most successful practitioners of pro-urgency are able to utilize their cognitive assets and their immensely powerful— if less visible—non-cognitive ones.

To master pro-urgency you must access and synthesize all of the conscious knowledge, inner "knowing," emotional understanding and other resources available to you at every level. If you develop this capacity and are committed to learning what you don't know, you:

> ➤ will be able to source virtually everything you need to function with proactive urgency;

> ➤ will be able to take actions with greater agility and decisiveness and without the need to discover, research and analyze every possible unknown element in a given scenario;

> ➤ will be able to stay in rapid, effective motion.

The following brief and non-scientific exploration uses words and phrases including *consciousness, intuition, association* and *levels of knowledge.* I have purposely elected to keep the discussion at the level of an overview.

What You Know.

On first reading, the quote below may sound a bit nonsensical or repetitive, but it is one of the best explanations of "levels of knowledge" that I have come across:

> Think of [a] circle . . . as containing all knowledge. The circle is divided into three sections.

> The first section of all knowledge is called, "What I know that I know." We all know what to do with what we know that we know—we put it to use.

> The next section of all knowledge is called, "What I know that I don't know." Again, we all know what to do with what we know that we don't know—we learn.

Finally, there is this vast remaining section of all knowledge called, "What I don't know that I don't know." What to do about what we don't know that we don't know is something of a dilemma. And, what we don't know that we don't know about human beings is an important question when it comes to individual and social transformation.[35]

When I first read this, I thought, "What in the world does that mean?" After reading it again a few times it sunk in, and I now appreciate it as a good framework for describing the universe of all knowledge.

© Nattavut

This sphere represents all levels of knowledge.
Imagine your mind in the middle of it.

The easy part of this is that we live in the land of what we know. We recognize everything and everybody. We have a good sense of where we are and what we are doing. This is our comfort zone. Check.

What You Don't Know.

Most of us eventually figure out that what we know is dwarfed by what we don't know. But we *do know* how to act on our curiosity and engage in the process of discovery. This can fill in the void of what we don't know and make the part of the circle containing *what we know* a bit larger. With continued inquiry and learning our comfort zone expands along with our knowledge.

Fortunately there are plenty of ways to learn what we don't know and update what we do. For the curious—and those electing to act with the power of urgency—locating answers (or at least very good starting points) is amazingly quick and easy. We all have access to communication devices that in an instant can take you almost anywhere in pursuit of your curiosity. There are no excuses for not being able to take that first step forward. Ask, and you will have a place to begin; the entire knowledge universe is at your disposal with the ubiquity and mass of the World Wide Web.

We daily move items of knowledge from one stack—what we don't know—to another: what we now do. It's all *in there* and *out there* somewhere, and you can get at it in many, many ways. You can bring to yourself what you require to fuel the actions you pursue with pro-urgency.

Somehow You Just Know.

As for not knowing what we don't know, this brings us back to accessing our non-cognitive resources. This requires an openness to discovering and relying upon the "I know it because I sense that I know it" part of our non-cognitive knowledge. The knowledge that is inside us but which is not neatly filed.

For example, when you are dealing with an unfamiliar situation or subject matter, a tool such as intuition can help move you in the right direction. Psychiatrist Carl Jung believed that intuitive access to ideas, concepts, possibilities and other ways out of a knowledge block are a result of *perceptions* rather than our logical thinking.

For this reason, you may not be able to figure out precisely why you are comfortable saying, "I am going to trust my intuition on this one," but more often than not you will be right. Your trust in yourself is rewarded as a good decision made without much effort required.

For our purposes, accurately describing intuition doesn't matter all that much. Even if we can't clearly explain how it works, it is still a ready resource. Its value lies in allowing us to access "knowing" in a manner that is not attributable to a discrete thought process. That is, we do not arrive at an intuitive understanding of a problem by logically thinking our way through it. Instead we just *know* and *feel it*, but with some degree of certainty.

We also use intuition to rapidly connect multiple elements of our prior learning and experience with what's in front of us at the moment. This helps us form a conceptual framework and a more cohesive plan of action. Who cares if we can't find the file folder from which our insights came or trace them back to their original sources?

Other Ways of Knowing.

The daily tidal wave of new information never ceases. Proactive personal power arises from our ability to *synthesize* what we learn from all sources, engage it and adapt it for our requirements at the moment—all in the same motion. And to do it continuously.

We use a variety of other tools and shortcuts, often without cognitive awareness. Some of these fall into the category of what are known as "heuristic" methods. The word "heuristic" may be a bit uncommon in daily conversation, but it describes methods of problem-solving with which all of us are familiar. Examples of heuristics include common sense, rules of thumb, educated guesses and trial-and-error.

One of the greatest benefits of using these tools is that they allow you to connect your immediate environment and experience with what you already know—without having to sort through an ever-growing stream of inputs in a logical, orderly fashion. Engaging and trusting these tools will accelerate your success with pro-urgency.

These kinds of shortcuts to decision making and action make up a good portion of your responses in a reactive, fight-or-flight moment. In that moment of extreme distress you may be unable to recognize *why* you know something of immediate value. You make sharp decisions without "knowing" in a linear sense, and you certainly don't have the luxury of "thinking it through." But you will latch onto and apply what comes up for you anyway without a heartbeat of hesitation.

These methods can be applied proactively to assist you with maintaining the intensity of your urgent efforts. Just as in the case of reactive urgency, you might be hard-pressed to say why you know what you know when you use these methods. But they often provide a confirmatory feeling like "It feels as though I'm moving in the right direction." With awareness and practice you can learn to call them into action as necessary—and quickly.

All of us utilize this mix of cognitive and more subtle resources to one extent or another. Mastery of achievement with proactive urgency requires a greater trust in the non-cognitive but very powerful knowing that is below the surface yet still readily accessible. All of us are quite capable of connecting and combining experience, cognition, and access to the various levels of consciousness. As mentioned above, you already do it. The trick as you move forward with pro-urgency is to simply become more aware of *when* you are doing it so you can be more purposeful in orchestrating and integrating all of your resources.[36]

Reach for More.

A way to frame how we access our non-obvious resources is by looking in on a basketball game. Think of a basketball court as a transparent rectangle in 3D. Each player on the court brings to it an awareness of the limitations of the space, their own capabilities and a knowledge of the ever-shifting geometric and spatial relationships they have with all of the other players.

In addition, each player is always aware of the location of the ball, baskets, coaches and referees, and of the dimension of time represented by the game clock. During the game the players continuously and almost without thinking make physical adjustments as required to fulfill their parts in making sure that when the horn sounds at the end of the game, their team has at least one point more than the opponent.

Professional athletes are terrific examples of real-time processors of information accessible through both top-of-mind, conscious-level awareness and that which resides within us as a deeper-level matrix of understanding and experience.37 This enables them to see situations that look familiar, even if they don't know precisely why. This in turn makes it easier to make rapid-fire decisions about what to do next.

What to spectators looks like a spontaneous decision leading to an unbelievable pass and dunk is actually action grounded in extensive experience gained from previous plays, including unsuccessful ones, and hundreds or thousands of mental playbacks.

Players do this not through rational thinking or intuition alone, but through a combination of the two, along with other heuristic methods. What happens as a result? The ball does what it is supposed to do: it goes in the basket.

It isn't as mysterious as it sounds. For example, have you ever been in a meeting and just had a sense that the group was uncomfortable and was waiting for someone to acknowledge it as a way of moving forward in the discussion?

The next time you are in this kind of situation, close your eyes if you can and simply try to feel the discomfort. See if something comes to mind in the form of knowledge (that you weren't aware was there) that gives you a starting point for addressing the sense of discomfort. Don't *think* it through, just open yourself to it. Expand your awareness. Something will come up.

If you can do this, you will have taken a step toward opening up access to the best of your personal power as a part of mastering conscious urgency.

You Do This Already.

No matter what analogy or example may work to assist you in understanding this process of accessing all of your individual resources, you are already doing it to one degree or another. There will be parts of this discussion that have resonated with you and some that did not. In speaking with a wide variety of people about these issues, many of them react with a statement like "I do this every day—I just haven't thought about these as tools I can manage proactively."

One of the best things you can do is trust in your own learning and experience applied to the circumstances and situations of today. If you actively and deliberately incorporate intuition and other heuristic tools into your assessment of the situation, you bring greater power and capacity to whatever you are pursuing.

Just as is the case with autopilot for planes, you have the ability to make continuous new and better judgments based on the feedback you receive as you speed through life. As fresh information and measurements come in you can immediately adjust a decision that was probably quite good when you first made it—and thereby update it to make it even better.[‡‡]

[‡‡] Also see Chapter 14: *Ongoing Inquiry—What Has Changed?*

Integration.

Learning how to access your full spectrum of available tools moves you from a position of constraint to one of possibility. You achieve freedom from the limitations of your history and create space for the possibilities of the future. In the process you drive the achievement of what you have determined to be your most important objectives.

I fully appreciate that this discussion leaves much unsaid. If you are interested in a deeper dive, there are many quality resources relating to consciousness, heuristics and the other elements referenced in this chapter. As mentioned above, knowledge is immediately accessible for the curious with access to an internet connection.

But remember—you don't *have* to learn more about the topic to begin putting it to use immediately. The good news is that you have been practicing this for years. You are the expert on *you* and how you work. Now it is simply a matter of being more aware and purposeful in accessing this storehouse of resources and personal power.

Urgency Rule #8

Your purposeful urgency can be fueled by the knowledge and sensory awareness you command at all levels of consciousness. Learn to rely upon your *sense of things* in addition to what you can objectively verify.

9

Distinction – See What You Need to See

Another powerful tool in your arsenal for creating with pro-urgency is your ability to utilize the benefits of distinctions.

A distinction is defined as a difference between two or more things, or—more importantly—the *recognition* of such a difference. For our purposes, I prefer this slightly nuanced definition: "A distinction is a difference that you have noticed or decided is important. Often used to separate things."[38]

In choosing to act with proactive urgency you must distinguish between what is relevant to your mission and what is not. You will then use that determination to guide your information gathering and actions as you move forward. If you are clear about your objective, this use of distinction will reveal what is necessary for its achievement. What you need to see and hear and do will begin to stand out in stark relief against the backdrop of infinite but amorphous possibilities.

Distinctions and Urgency – Reactive and Proactive.

A flight-or-flight situation very rapidly propels both your body and mind into an altered state. In Chapter 2 we addressed what happens with your body in such a situation, including a flush of hormones to your system and increased blood flow to your muscles. In the case of your mind, an immediate, stark distinction is drawn between the imminent threat and everything else.

In such states you can literally only see and feel the threat in all of its intensity. As to the rest of the world, you might as well be wearing blinders. You are suddenly transported into a state of highly selective awareness where the stuff that will help you deal with the immediate threat becomes bigger than life.

As this process takes place you discover that the small bits of information you have instantly captured are so germane that they can be turned into very rapid—and potentially lifesaving—decisions and actions.

It is the same with proactive urgency. You can actively create distinctions that help you gather and process the available information and resources required to move toward your objective. If this kind of mental filtering wasn't powerful, it wouldn't be in the mix of things designed to protect you from harm in fight-or-flight situations. It is available to you now.

Isolating the Relevant.

Most of the time, we observe a sea of indistinct inputs flowing over, around and through our senses.

You have the opportunity to turn the powerful tool of distinction to purposeful use at your discretion. You can accomplish this by using your reasoning rather than waiting for the rush you would experience in a confrontation with danger.

Creating distinctions will highlight the concepts, ideas, information, knowledge and other data potentially relevant to your important priorities. Their use will also allow the irrelevant to simply wash over you.

If you decide your business must launch its new product faster than any competitor ever has, you can create a distinction. "What have other companies done to accelerate the process of product launches?" I promise that everyone on your team will soon begin to bring to the conversation example after example from a wide variety of sources of the ways others have approached and gained experience from the same kind of challenge. This effort will open the door to possibilities perhaps never before considered.

When we create distinctions between the things we really care about in the torrent of all the unfiltered input we receive, the former suddenly pop out with such clarity that we wonder how we previously missed them. They were, in fact, hidden in plain sight until we infused them with special significance.

The more precise you can be in crafting a distinction, the more powerful the impact you will have on the things that matter to you most. You may have heard the term "fine distinction." As you master pro-urgency, the use of finely drawn distinctions will enable you to discover with a higher degree of specificity what you need to satisfy your requirements.

Powerful and Uncomplicated.

Consider the games children play in the car when traveling: find the numbers from one to a hundred, find things that are yellow, find things beginning with the letters in the alphabet, starting with "A," and so on.

If you did this as a kid, you probably remember that you would instantaneously find an incredible richness of "what needed to be seen" in order to take the next step in the game. Without introducing the concept of distinction you would simply have seen the landscape passing by indistinctly, and probably been bored because of it.

Look around you now and find things that are in pairs (two of anything). Were you conscious of them before I asked you to distinguish them from their surroundings?

Here's another one: How many times was the word "find" used in the previous paragraphs in this section? Once you've been asked the question, if you go back and look you cannot avoid seeing all five of them, almost as if they were the only words there.

Let me share a personal example, something that came about as I was considering and then writing this book about the power of urgency. Once I settled on the central idea, I created a distinction between things even potentially related to my subject and everything else.

I began to see and hear examples of urgency in all of its forms in news reports, conversations, magazine articles and television shows, even when I wasn't specifically looking for them. I couldn't have ignored them if I wanted to.

The same thing would happen at night when all of a sudden I would get a sentence in my head, cutting through the other brain activity, which perfectly expressed a concept I had previously found difficult to articulate. It was as if once I gave my brain the assignment of finding information about urgency, it was on-task 24/7. The power of distinction is active even while you are sleeping.

© Jahina Photography

One at a time: Find the rectangles.
Find the triangles. Find the squares.

There is incredible power in using distinction as a tool to connect you to the information relevant for accomplishing your most important goals. Consider distinction to be the practical version of the law of attraction—without having to refer to quantum physics or indulge in large helpings of dense gobbledygook.

This level of heightened awareness is both powerful and easy to employ in your service. Jonathan Swift said, "Vision is the art of seeing what is invisible to others."[39]

You've got everything you need.

Simply define the things you want to see and hear more than anything else. And they will find you.

Urgency Rule #9

There is power, clarity and efficiency in creating and consciously attending to distinctions. You can see what you need to see, when you need to see it.

10

<u>Waiting for Perfection</u>

Really successful people not only want "it"—they want it *now*.

More accurately they want to be in hot pursuit of it now, because they can then be in motion, pushing in the direction of something of importance to them. There is *life* in the cause they have selected for themselves.

People who want it now commit to doing whatever is necessary to advance their own cause—and to doing it *post haste*. They are not considering, thinking about, studying or in any other way procrastinating it. They have gotten ready, aimed, and are already firing. They know something that the rest of us may not know or have forgotten.

Choosing to be urgent in your current state of being means embracing "you" as you are now and moving into action. There is no different or better you that you must become before you can take the first step in the direction of achieving your significant objectives.

The real difference between people who are already in motion and those who are stuck lies in the understanding that the only perfect moment for action... is this one.

If Only...

Consider these types of excuses for standing still: "If only I was better educated about business I could really go after a job I would enjoy." Or, "If only I was in better shape I could pursue the kind of job that requires some degree of physical activity."

It is quite possible to spend so much of your life pursuing peripheral changes—the kind you think are necessary preparation for what you *really* want to do—that you never get around to simply doing the things that will get you into action.

Consider this argument: "If only I wasn't a procrastinator, I know I could be a star at work. I'm almost ready to deal with my tendency to procrastinate, and then I will be ready to be a manager. I just don't want to be a manager until I quit smoking, which I could do whenever I want to... but then I will probably gain more weight. If that happens, I will have to buy some new clothes. Of course, if I bought new clothes it would look like I was trying to be a show-off, like the guy who's manager now. A lot of people resent him, and I don't want to be resented."

As we grow up, most of us seem to absorb the idea that all of our so-called imperfections are prospects for change. We feel that once we improve or eradicate these perceived flaws—then we *really* will be ready to unlock the future we've dreamed of. Then, and only then, will we be ready to get into action.

Unfortunately, too many of us go through life waiting for perfection while the starting line continues to move away from us. We use a lot of the above-referenced "if only's" along with several helpings of "when/then" equations to avoid taking even the first step in the direction of what would be required to make "it" happen.

What Do You (Really) Want?

On we go through our lives, deferring the pursuit of goals that could be powerfully transformative for us. We believe we somehow must be in a state other than our current one before we can truly begin. This belief keeps us both stuck and using our precious energy comparing where we are with where we think we need to be. We willingly spend our time deferring action instead of opening up to actively creating our future with what we already possess.

You may recognize this type of inner chatter: "I realize I'm a circle, but I'm not satisfied. If only I could become a triangle I know my life would be better."

So you work and work to change into the triangle you have now determined to become. When you are almost finished with your reshaping, your best friend says, "I've been thinking about your wanting to become a triangle and I think you would be much better off as a square. If you were a square, I bet you could really go places."

You reply, "Hmm... I think you may be right," and off you go to discover what you need to do to be your better, square self. And so in search of whatever it is we think we need to be in order to look and be perfect (or at least better than we are) at the starting line, we end up turning ourselves into pretzels.

We even torture those around us because we know so much about change as a catalyst for being better human beings that of course we want to share it: "If only you, my love, were more social, we would have more friends and fun in our lives. I know you can change this one little thing for me and, most of all, for you! You'll be perfect!"

Imperfect?

By your own and other people's definitions you probably really are incredibly imperfect. You may see yourself as shallow, uncaring, selfish, apathetic, faking it or at least disingenuous. You might at times look inside and recognize similarities to someone who is angry, weak and fearful of being found out. These perceptions—fair or unfair—may lead you to postpone things that, in your view, require a better *you* to even initiate them.

The truth is that no matter how you view your shortcomings, no matter how harshly you describe yourself, *if you are waiting to live your life until you can change yourself for the better—don't bother*.

Start living it now.

Why?

Waiting to live until conditions are ideal, or even just improved, means never getting in the game. In fact, once you deal with your current imperfections there is no doubt you will identify new ones. Trying to keep up with and correct them before engaging in true action toward the goals that matter is a downward spiral without end.

For a good portion of my life I sought to change who I was into someone different. I was sure that if I was different I would surely be better. I was convinced that who I was at the time was inadequate to accomplish what I then viewed as the really important things in life.

If only I had a college degree, a law degree, a master's degree, spoke a foreign language and had lived abroad. *If only* I had more experience in business, more money, was less of an introvert, was more confident, less rigid, more relaxed, et cetera, et cetera, *ad infinitum*, THEN *everything would be possible.* I pursued all of these things and "fixed" many of them. No doubt I was becoming ever more accomplished and *now* was *almost* ready to take to the *starting* line!

© Bob Coglianese

Perfection in the Moment: Secretariat and Ron Turcotte.

But this pursuit ignored two very important things.

First, my real and immediately accessible life was passing me by. Instead of embracing it, I was taking the long way around by pursuing change that would, I hoped, take me to the better life waiting for me when I became a more perfect version of me.

And second, no matter how much effort I put into this kind of change, it turned out that I was still pretty much the same old me. I might have had a new degree or skill, but if I kept waiting to act based on standards of perfection, it was clear that the starting line for my "real" life would remain forever distant.

The Moment Has Arrived.

Let's be honest. One fear we can probably put aside forever is that we will never attain perfection. Fortunately, life really isn't about approaching such an impossible standard.

Try this instead: "I am as I am—imperfections and all. If I choose to improve my mind and body, shift my thinking or add to my experiences, I will do so because I *choose* these things. I don't need to pursue them in order to be a more "perfect" me than the one I already am."

I suspect you have a lot of fuel languishing in your tank in the form of personal power. Realize that your engine *is what it is* and is perfect without modification. Top off your tank and step on the accelerator.

You also certainly don't need to wait until your negative self-talk about all these things goes away (it won't, at least for a while). In fact, you're far better off if you simply stop waiting for *anything*.

You *are* already. Just. Go.

This is what successful people know and never forget.

You can expend your energy in pursuit of your good cause right now rather than rationalizing why it is important to wait until you can be a better shape, color, design or overall human being.

If you want to keep suffering and blaming your "imperfections," you certainly can. But, take a moment to appreciate these questions from Werner Erhard:

If not you, who?

If not now, when?

If not here, where?

Urgency Rule #10

The future of a moment ago has arrived. You bring to it your perfection along with your uniqueness. Make it your mission to leverage your uniqueness starting immediately.

11

There is No "Playing It Safe"

In the preceding chapters you were introduced to many of the foundational elements of proactive urgency. In addition to the Urgency Rules offered at the end of each of the chapters, here is a brief review of some of the key points from Part One:

1. A sense of urgency can be proactively created. It can be practiced and perfected.

2. Urgency-by-choice is purposeful, insistent, committed action pursued with a passionate edge.

3. Proactive urgency is being accessed when you choose cool, clear, energetic and sustainable passion to get what is worthy of your best efforts.

4. Purposeful urgency represents a lower voltage version of the extreme edge and single-minded focus we have when acting with the reactive urgency prompted by a crisis, emergency or dangerous confrontation.

5. Moving one step beyond your comfort zone takes you into the promised land of the discomfort zone— where anything is possible.

6. Conscious urgency is not merely going faster, nor is it simply time-management. It is the relentless pursuit of something that can be game-changing for you.

7.   Any potential risk in taking thoughtful, urgent action is almost always overstated. Unfortunately, this fact often doesn't become clear until after an opportunity has evaporated.

8.   Self-reliance is an antidote to the declining strength of external institutions and paradigms. It represents a purposeful shift to working from the inside out.

9.   Your apparent weaknesses are often simply strengths in disguise. Ask the question, "What is the flip side of what I see as weakness? If I was forced to characterize it as something positive, what would I say about it?"

10. Acting with proactive urgency can deliver at least a 1% advantage on a consistent basis. This will lead you to regularly outperform your expectations and reach the objectives you set for yourself.

11. Choosing to create with urgency can drive "faster, better, cheaper" for any organization.

12. You have found the essence of purposeful urgency when you put more energy into something than is required to do it.

13. The experience and wisdom you possess at all levels of consciousness is readily accessible. Trust the tools and shortcuts you have to mine these assets, and engage them with purpose.

14. In the use of distinctions you will discover what you need, when you need it, in the service of your important objectives.

15. The perfect state from which to move into action with urgency-by-choice is represented by who you

are, where you are and what you have at this moment.

If you already possess a level of expertise and achievement through your practice of something similar to proactive urgency, the preceding pages have likely reminded you of at least some of what you already know. If you don't have experience intentionally using urgency to drive your actions, you now have a framework for leveraging your uniqueness, time and effort in the pursuit of your most important objectives. More about this is just ahead in Part Two.

Being Safe.

Choosing urgency to change your game requires a mindset of full engagement and continuous action. As a consequence of this it will necessarily *feel unsafe* from time-to-time.

We go to great lengths to create a sense of safety for ourselves and the most important people in our lives. There is nothing wrong with this, and a lot right about it. But strip away the insulating layers and justifications for why you are not at risk relating to potential threats of all kinds and you will find an unavoidable truth:

There is no place of certain safety.

Yet we decorate our comfort zones as though they are permanent residences. And we go much further. We procrastinate and justify and defend the status quo with a misplaced belief that accepting default outcomes is safer than taking purposefully selected actions and getting into motion. We study, defer and create contingency plans. We buy life insurance, create circles of trust and even purchase preplanned and pre-paid funerals. We work at developing backstops of all kinds.

But none of the above (nor *anything* you can add to it) makes anyone truly safe or fearless.

One of my favorite quotes about safety and security is from Helen Keller. She wrote, "Security is mostly a superstition. It does not exist in nature, nor do the children of men as a whole experience it. Avoiding danger is no safer in the long run than outright exposure. Life is either a daring adventure or nothing."[40]

As a deaf and blind person she had plenty of reasons to avoid even the most basic risks in life, let alone those involved in taking on challenges requiring tremendous boldness and strength of will. She could have folded up early in life and played it safe. Instead she found the courage to live life as a daring adventure, and the world is a better place because of her commitment.

Acting with purposeful urgency requires accepting the risks of *doing*. Since we are all at risk anyway, why not embrace these risks as mere challenges on the path to our most important objectives? And then aggressively manage them to minimize any potential downside? Since safety is an illusion, simply say, "I am not feeling very safe and secure at the moment—I must be *living!*"

Onward.

Urgency Rule #11

Security is mainly illusory. Remember Helen Keller's words: "Avoiding danger is typically no safer in the long run than outright exposure." Practice leaving your comfort zone.

PART TWO

Playing to Win
with
The Power of Urgency

ACT.

"It is important that you get clear for yourself that your only access to impacting life is action.

The world does not care what you intend, how committed you are, how you feel, or what you think, and certainly it has no interest in what you want and don't want.

Take a look at life as it is lived and see for yourself that the world only moves for you when you act."

~ Werner Erhard

Part Two – Introduction
The "A-Game" System

Proactive urgency is a dynamic system driven by assessment, action, and adaptation based upon feedback as you strive to reach your goals. You are the *synthesizer* of the elements of your actively managed urgency system on a continuous, seamless basis. The building blocks are:

- ✓ **A**ctive Commitment.
- ✓ **A**bsolute Truth.
- ✓ **A**ssessment and Continuous Adjustments.
- ✓ **A**daptation and Problem Solving.
- ✓ **A**lleviating Fears.
- ✓ **A**ll In.

This is what I call the "A-Game" System. I chose the term "A-Game" to reflect engagement of the best we have to offer in pursuit of what we choose to focus on with pro-urgency. The above points encompass the elements of the proactive urgency process in the shortest possible summary. The individual elements of the A-Game are more fully addressed sequentially in the remaining chapters.

The pro-urgency process once launched is a fluid, dynamic system in which you respond and adapt to immediate circumstances and feedback. You are the systems monitor of all the variables that are in play.

You pay attention to both what you *know* and what you *feel* regarding the requirements and adjustments that are necessary. You continuously evaluate "what is" and "what needs to be." You do this as much as possible in a state of openness and anticipation rather than response.

The illustrations I offer in the succeeding chapters are largely based on my work as a change agent and catalyst for businesses, managers and leaders committed to urgently changing the status quo. I also know firsthand that pro-urgency works just as well for achieving non-business objectives. Whether in work or life in general, embracing pro-urgency is *playing to win* when it counts most for you.

12

Acts, Not Words – Commitment and Authenticity

(Active Commitment)

All of the foundational elements for acting with pro-urgency are "free" in the sense that you already possess them. It is your choice to turn such passive assets into active ones. You can transform a wandering approach to your key goals into a focused framework for directed action. This very day you are as qualified as anyone in the world to pursue and get what you want through a pro-urgent effort which you create where you are with what you have.

As with everything of value, though, there is a price to be paid for achieving what you want. In the case of proactive urgency as a way of pursuing game-changing goals of all kinds, there is only one universal currency accepted: *complete commitment* to the process.

A *pro-urgent commitment* is a sustained, continuously-renewed promise manifested in your actions. Pro-urgent actions without this commitment are unsustainable.

As succinctly stated by Jean-Paul Sartre, "Commitment is an act, not a word." It is not enough to *say* you are committed, no matter how fervently you declare it. Only actions express the truth and the depth of your commitment.

This kind of unequivocal commitment is the stock-in-trade of powerful mothers and fathers, business builders, entrepreneurs, job creators, game changers and high performers in every field of endeavor.

When we truly commit, we give ourselves a gift: the ability to sustain a high level of urgency until our results are achieved or—for our own reasons—we abandon the objective.

At a deeper level, to bring forth the best of yourself in the service of your pro-urgent effort you must also accept responsibility for the status quo in your life—and for your ability to change it. This necessitates consistently declaring, delivering on and renewing your commitment to the objective, the process and yourself as both creator *and* actor.

The Most Powerful You.

The first step of this journey involves taking stock of the state of the vehicle you will use to manage the urgency-by-choice process through to the achievement of your objective. The vehicle is *you.*

Acting with conscious urgency can't involve denying or hiding from your true self. Achieving your goals requires serious commitment and focus. You cannot compromise at the starting gate. This is commonly called a "false start' and with good reason.

Commitment in pro-urgency terms requires being as true to who you really are as you can get.

I suggest that the most powerful version of you lives in alignment with your beliefs, thoughts, actions and words. It is you acting with purpose and independence of thought and action. It is you unafraid to present as "authentic"—the unadulterated version of who you are—in the pursuit of what you want, and to do so consistently.

Harvard Professor Chris Argyis writes in *Teaching Smart People How to Learn*, "Put simply, people consistently act inconsistently, unaware of the contradiction . . . between the way they think they are acting, and the way they really act."[41]

His colleague, Michael Jensen, adds, "If you watch carefully in life, you will have the opportunity to catch yourself being small [inconsistent and inauthentic] . . . While you won't like seeing this, by distinguishing these weaknesses in yourself, you will give yourself a powerful opportunity to master these weaknesses. One cannot *pretend* to be authentic. That, by definition, is inauthentic."[42]

I am drawing the line between authenticity and inauthenticity sharply in order to make the distinction clear. Take a look at how much of your life has been spent caring about what other people think, both in general terms and more specifically *about you*. You are not alone; we have all done it. But caring about what other people think reveals the *inauthentic* in you—the part that is afraid of being seen for who you really are.

You can simply choose, starting now, to gradually shift in the direction of caring *more* about your own alignment and less about what others think it should be. A good place to start might be to observe what others seem to *want you to be* and simply try to understand what motivates their apparent desire. Opening this inquiry will allow you to learn something about yourself and them, and to begin caring—at least a little bit less—about how others perceive you.

Here are a few examples of behaviors that represent inauthenticity:

➤ You remain silent when you feel strongly about an issue and really should make your opinion known.

➤ You trade away your integrity for a fleeting moment of looking good.

➤ You restrain yourself when you can stand up for a friend or colleague—you are disloyal.

➤ You stand by and wait for someone else to act with compassion when you observe a child or animal in distress.

Have you ever found yourself acting in ways similar to these in comparable circumstances? Did you behave the way you did at the time for any reason other than that you wanted to be perceived as different from who you really are?

Ask yourself: If you are fighting for an objective that matters to you, why would you permit strangers (or even well-meaning people close to you) to determine or influence your future by seeking or simply awaiting their approval?

This is what you are doing when you remain silent or knowingly engage in actions against your interests.

"What Do You Think of Me?"

My good friend and colleague Michael Donati[43] related an experience that is a striking example of the difference between personal authenticity and everything else.

After a number of difficult years of marriage his wife was diagnosed with multiple personality disorder. She was told that caring for their three children and dealing with her relationship with Michael was making her condition worse. Because of her mental challenges, she wasn't in a position to make a rational judgment about what to do. This was left to Michael.

He wanted to do the right thing by her and their children. At the same time, he didn't want to be—or be perceived by his children as—the kind of person who would abandon his wife and their mother in a time of obvious need. He wasn't such a man, yet he felt at the time that not only his children but the "community at large" might view him as a heartless scoundrel if he parted ways with her.

Michael met with a psychiatrist to get yet another opinion. He explained the situation and told the doctor that he really wanted to stay married to his wife. He asked for advice as to how that might be possible.

The doctor asked him a single question: "Given your wife's severe multiple personality disorder, is there any circumstance under which you can see your marriage to her working out for all concerned, especially your children?"

It was a question that left Michael no room to hide. Given the enormous consequences of his decision for himself and his loved ones, he had to answer as his true self.

After a very long pause he answered, "No."

As of that moment, the issue was complete for his children, his wife and himself. He had embraced his personal authenticity. He didn't hide. He didn't take an unrealistically optimistic position that might have made him appear "heroic" but which would have glossed over the reality he was facing. In answering "no" he was acting as the owner of his life and actions. He welcomed this new perspective and has lived it continuously since.

Today if someone asks him, "What do you think of me?" his answer will likely be a more gently stated version of

"I *don't* think of you." You also won't hear him ask, "Do you like me?" or anything similar to it, because whether you like him or not is simply irrelevant to him.

I should also say that his life's work is being of service to others. There is no contradiction between being a fierce warrior fully committed to your highest purpose, acting with authenticity *and* serving others with the best of yourself.

Acting with pro-urgency requires getting as close to the unadulterated truth of a situation—and ourselves—as we possibly can. What is objectively true? What is not? These kinds of inquiries must be made when you are thinking and acting as close to your authentic state of being as humanly possible.

This means leaving the contest for most admired, best liked or most popular to others.

Conformity and Consensus.

Acting with objectivity and authenticity is always harder than rolling with the tides of convention—into which you can certainly disappear. But your willingness to be a selective non-conformist is where the creation of your future begins. A willingness to see and act upon alternative or perhaps unpopular points of view means you are plugging into the part of you that plans to *achieve*, through proactive urgency and otherwise, and not—simply—*try*.

Even if you work to escape it, there will always be hands clutching at you from out of the crowd with the intention of pulling you back to where they think you belong. It takes courage to not conform, to be true to yourself.

© Roy McKeown

Find the nonconformist.

Some leaders believe that management by consensus is effective because a proposed strategy, objective or tactic is supported by broad and visible buy-in and support. There is no doubt it is possible for a consensus to represent real commitment on the part of those involved.

But more often than not, consensus is a form of rubber-stamp-like conformity masquerading as an agreement of independent thinkers. The reasons for the consensus often have nothing to do with real commitment. Apparent support for consensus can merely be a manifestation of peer pressure, a desire for favor with the boss, groupthink dynamics, fear of all flavors and many other things. It often has nothing to do with honest support for an idea or situation upon which everyone actually agrees.

In fact, a consensus can be an indicator of feelings of vulnerability among employees, rather than a real agreement signifying collective commitment. The story with the punch line "I don't have to outrun the bear, I just have to outrun you!" comes to mind. In a herd of antelope being hunted by a cheetah, you don't want to be the one that is ill or slow that day, or you'll be dinner. In many business organizations the perception is that you don't want to be the one to break with consensus—or you might be pushed out of the herd.

Late decisions arrived at after a time-chewing process of consensus-building will be of little solace when your company is eviscerated in the marketplace. Consensus-building might provide the illusion of safety based on a historical context of change in increments. But waiting for the weakest links in your organization to "get with the program" is far from a best practice today. When your business is in the crypt along with countless others, nobody will care if you are able to equitably allocate responsibility for the failure in just the right measures.

Andy Grove, longtime Intel CEO, writes, "Most companies don't die because they are wrong; most die because they don't commit themselves. They fritter away their valuable resources while attempting to make a decision. The greatest danger is in standing still."[44]

If you are feeling bulletproof due to the collegial, consensus-oriented culture you are overseeing, it might only be because the bullets haven't yet pierced your buildings or have thus far missed you.

The bloodletting simply may not have begun.

Shrink or Grow.

Your authentic commitment is a required, deliberate step into ownership of a process you have chosen to pursue with urgency. Our world today, and that of the future, increasingly depends upon those committed souls who tap into ownership as their *modus operandi*. Ultimately, the choice of mindset is one of shrink or grow. If you choose a path of urgent creation in your life, all of the resources and experiences you have (and in the case of the latter, have ever had) will come into alignment in support of your journey of achievement.

Each of us possesses a unique collection of assets and resources, with some blessed in one area and others in another. But we all can make the choice to be owners, to be true to ourselves and use what we *do* have in proactive and efficient ways.

You have the option of accepting full ownership of your life and rejecting being on the receiving end of other people's decisions—at least for the things that count. What could that degree of commitment mean for you?

Urgency Rule #12

A purposeful commitment to acting with pro-urgency is a sustained, continuously renewed promise manifested in your bold actions. This ongoing promise leaves no room for fakery, conformity or false consensus.

13

What Is True?

(Absolute Truth)

"There are only two mistakes one can make along the road to truth; not going all the way, and not starting." So said Buddha.

Difficult though it may be, the assessment of "what is true"—both initially and as it shifts based on actions and results—is the most powerful tool you have for making decisions that comport with reality. Whether you like the assessment as it unfolds makes no difference whatsoever. Answering the question "What is true?" with objectivity is all that matters.

"Where Am I Going?"

Ask yourself: "What do I want that is worthy of my committed, urgent effort?" Your answer should describe the future-perfect state of what you *will have created* as you look back on your journey to the achievement. As much as possible, your vision should be devoid of wishes, hopes, speculations, and unrealistic contingencies.[45] It should represent a choice made by you with all of the authenticity you can muster. "This is what I want." It should accurately describe in detail "what will be" as you envision it.

It is not a process of visualization and attraction. If you happen to get an assist from the Invisible Hand of the Universe, take it and consider it a bonus.

Never stop working on actively describing what your future-perfect state will be. Your assessments and the exact words you use needn't be perfect. As with everything related to proactive urgency, the purpose isn't perfection. The value lies in the thinking that goes into the creation and, perhaps more importantly, the actions and revisions along the way.

"What is True Today?"

Just as important as a thoughtful articulation of your objective is the evaluation of the present state of things—the status quo. If you want to review the choices you made previously, simply examine your present. Your current state is a perfect reflection of your prior decisions. By the same token, if you want to know your future, the actions you take now will create it.

The starting point for engaging pro-urgency in earnest is getting as close as you can to an objective view of "what is true now." Your initial task is to evaluate all information of possible relevance to the circumstances representing the current status quo. This is the case whether your goal is personal, business or social.

Your degree of commitment to this evaluation indicates just how intensely immersed you have chosen to be in the process leading to the achievement of your objective. This is putting the "wood behind the arrow"—focusing single-mindedly on what you have identified as worthy of your time and attention. Your highest current purpose.

As you will soon see, there is nothing you can conclude from your initial assessment that you cannot revise as new inputs and facts unfold. Nothing is static. The greatest challenge—and the most powerful guarantor of success—

involves engaging this process of evaluation consistently and in a truly effective way.

During this discovery effort, it is okay to be out of balance or even *in extremis*[46] for a while in order to completely commit yourself to the course you have chosen.

In most cases, an assessment of "what is true" will necessarily include observations and inputs from others. In a business context this is not only valuable but unavoidable. These inputs will vary in accuracy and value. They will also have attached to them individual filters resulting from the same kinds of experiences, assumptions and biases that color your own interpretations.

If you trust any of these inputs without interrogation and verification you may find yourself at a starting point based mostly on half-truths and someone else's subjective reality.

It takes extraordinary effort to get to the *true* truth. Most people will stop before they get there. As they see their comfort zone dissolve around them they will start to think, "I can't" or "I won't." This can especially be the case if digging for the truth puts you out of synch with the comfort zones of others.

A bias toward collegiality and comfort in your assessment of the status quo is typically not helpful when acting with urgency-by-choice. In fact, such a bias is often an indicator of a stagnant status quo.

Leave the saccharine and rose-colored filters for the things you *wish* or *hope* to achieve, rather than those you won't be denied.

Forensic Methods.

In finding the required truths to move your quest forward, think of yourself as running your own forensic lab. Although the science of forensics is usually associated with the criminal justice system, it is a perfect model for discovering and understanding the environment that forms the starting point for any serious effort undertaken with proactive urgency.

Most of us have seen enough television shows involving crime, criminals, labs, detectives and prosecutors to know there are two main types of evidence. The first type is *direct* evidence in the form of a confession, eyewitness testimony or perhaps a video recording of a crime. Each of these may be subject to challenge, but at face value they are given great weight.

The other type of evidence is *circumstantial.* DNA, fingerprints and handwriting authentication. This evidence can associate a person with a crime, but will require additional contextual information and reasoning in order to connect the dots to a conviction.

In your commitment to objectivity, use both direct and circumstantial findings to create your initial assessment and to provide ongoing feedback for making course corrections.

Extracting the truth from a given situation is the best way to create a solid foundation for your efforts. Seek, find, review and process everything you can discover of potential relevance. See it as solving a mystery—with the achievement of your goal as the ultimate, wholly satisfying and unsurprising ending.

A Bias for Action.

You may have seen the unique television show *House* featuring the irascible and brilliant Dr. Gregory House.[47] His unusual methods of medical investigation offer another insight into how to launch and sustain a pro-urgent effort.

One of the mainstay parts of the storyline in most episodes is the tension between Dr. House and the team of doctors that supports him. As he is the "chief," he seeks the analyses and opinions of those around him. In most cases, the junior doctors want to pursue a sequential course of treatment based upon the "hard" evidence of lab tests and reports until a specific diagnosis and treatment is proven appropriate or not.

But there is a cost for this sequential approach: time. Often the esoteric and unusual medical conditions that come to the attention of the physicians require immediate action. The loss of time can mean regression in the health of the patient and even death. This is where Dr. House's experience and his use of distinction come to the rescue.

Responding to a situation in which a diagnostic test will take hours or days to give a result, Dr. House will say something to the effect of, "If we wait for the test, the patient will die in the meantime. Let's treat this as if we already know it is *pantothenate kinase-associated neurodegeneration*."[48]

Dr. House chooses to trust his foundation of knowledge, his deductive reasoning, his use of fine distinctions and his instincts. He keeps the process moving to keep the patient alive while still driving the forensic effort to determine the root cause of the illness.

The use of *rational assumptions until they are proven false* is a powerful tool to maintain direction and speed toward your objective. Use the information at your disposal but have a bias in favor of actions presumed to be correct. Permit no loss of velocity or momentum. But also be highly vigilant in your efforts to validate your assumptions as you gain fresh information and insights.

More is Better.

In my work in rapid transformation for businesses and committed individuals, the first step in the direction of creating with urgency is getting a clear view of both historical and current circumstances. The immediate conditions will dictate the type of data, how much of it can be accessed and how fast it must be digested. I consider this the raw material for acting with pro-urgency.

Here is an example. Not long ago I received a call from a company's principal investors. They asked me to make a rapid assessment of the business and offer my recommendations. There was a catch, though. In this particular case I would not be able to interview any of the current management or other key personnel. It is always preferable to have conversations with the people who have been "driving the bus." It isn't always possible, because the questions needing answers might prove disruptive and reveal investor concerns before the time is right.

The first step was to learn everything I could about the company through means other than conversations with the people in it. I made a list of the information that I thought would give me a pretty complete picture of what was happening in the company. I requested financial statements, business plans, monthly and quarterly reports, trend and organization charts, bios of key personnel, product and service offerings and the sales and marketing materials to support them, customer lists, consulting reports, competitive data, online or public reporting information, news articles, and whatever else was available. I ended up receiving the digital files and paper equivalent of several large cardboard boxes of materials in response.

© TFoxFoto

I love the expression "drinking from the fire hydrant" to describe those occasions when it is necessary to absorb and process a lot of information in very short order. For me, there is something invigorating about rapid learning. But even if you aren't as thrilled as I might be at the prospect of reviewing large amounts of information, acting with pro-urgency *will* require immersion in the process.

In this case, I reviewed everything that had been sent along to me—some items more thoroughly than others (based upon my experience and a sense of what was redundant as the process progressed). Certain pieces of information offered more insights than others and better helped me connect the dots in order to piece together the whole. This process was facilitated by trusting in the kinds of knowing that were the subject of Chapter 8: *Consciousness—You Know What You Need to Know.*

I developed a list of questions to be answered by the investors and several former employees. I also recognized a need for further research into the industry, its trends, developments and notable players. I reviewed the resumes and biographical information of the key people in the company and discovered more information in the trails left on social media sites.

When I engage in this process I fully enter the dynamic of the business. I mentally triangulate what I see "is" today—the immediate situation—as well as what opportunities are or may be available, including an assessment of what competitors are doing. I open my consciousness to work in what I call "background mode"49–twenty-four hours a day—awake or asleep. Bit-by-bit, likely conclusions bubble up and are captured. The picture comes into view.

This part of the process involves for me a form of intense immersion such that I can find meaningful answers to questions including, *What would I do if I owned this business? What actions would I take and in what order would I take them so as to protect my investment and optimize the outcome?* I assume an owner's mentality and apply my experience and unique point of view. I bring a high degree of objectivity to the situation. I always ask, *How would I react if I had to follow my own recommendations?*

In the case of this particular company, when I reached this point, I felt I had arrived at a rational assessment of the current state of the business. I wrote a short summary of my approach, assessment, conclusions and recommendations and set up a call with the investors to review it. We went forward from there and mutually committed to implement my recommendations through a continuing collaboration.

I decided to work with them because of their own level of commitment to the success of the venture. This was important to me, because today I choose only to work with people who are truly all-in as it relates to our joint efforts. I want to spend my life in the service of others, with people and businesses who want to create something great with the time and resources at their disposal. I don't want to offer up my best in a wishy-washy situation with people who won't or can't commit. As has been repeated here ad nauseam, making a commitment and continuously renewing it is essential for success with applied urgency.

The same is true of my work with individuals. In these cases, the forensic challenge of determining the truth is pursued for the most part through conversation rather than written or digital reports and documentation. The objective, however, is identical. What circumstances, decisions and actions led to today's status quo? Is this person committed to creating a shift in their life or business? How do we urgently and productively go forward from here?

These same questions are the ones you need to ask of yourself when engaging in action with pro-urgency, whether for your business or other enterprise, or for you as an individual.

It is not necessary to completely understand and process every word and number, every circumstance and situation. This is impossible. Furthermore, each part of an interview or conversation will not carry the same significance. Nonetheless, the process is integral to creating a conceptual framework for your course ahead. As you fill out this framework, you can apply to it distinction, intuition and other tools and perspectives based on the levels of consciousness and experience you bring to the effort.

Gradually, a more comprehensive picture will emerge from the facts and circumstances being discovered. This provides a foundation for asking more questions and getting to the rationale underlying the actions previously taken.

In your individual efforts with proactive urgency, this engagement is represented as a commitment to being a knowledge seeker—to being insatiably curious about anything that relates to the pursuit of your objective. What could be more important than becoming a master of all that is relevant to your achievement? What better use could you make of your time?

The forensic clues are always present in any information. You will recall that in some television crime dramas and reality shows the investigators even go through the trash. One man's trash....

Welcome being inundated with everything relevant to your cause. It is the fuel you need to achieve your goal through your pro-urgent effort. Be curious—on steroids—for the information that matters to you. Remember the use of distinction: what do you want or need to see more than anything else?

The Truth Is Out There.

To harness the power of urgency-by-choice in the most effective manner possible, your assessment of the problem or objective at hand must be as close to 20/20 accuracy as you can get. This assessment is what informs your first steps toward your goal, so it only makes sense to begin on as sure footing as possible.

But it is equally important that you continue to revise and update your assessment and consequent actions based on real-world feedback. This requirement is addressed in the next chapter. The more you or those around you are willing to lie or distort the truth, the further afield your steps will take you from your goal—and from accessing the true power of acting with pro-urgency.

It takes objectivity and courage to a degree not typically seen in order to maintain your perspective and velocity in acting with pro-urgency. And why shouldn't it? You are shifting from trying to doing.

Urgency Rule #13

Set your goal to pursue with proactive urgency with as much clarity and descriptiveness as you can. Be ruthlessly objective in assessing the totality of the environment and conditions that exist at the starting line for your effort. Gather, review and digest all of the information that is available.

14

<u>Ongoing Inquiry – What Has Changed?</u>

(**A**ssessment and Continuous Adjustments)

You have created a vibrant description of what your future perfect will be when you have achieved your objective.

You have made an unequivocal commitment to its achievement and you have embraced a passionate "edge" in your approach to the process.

You have evaluated your starting position with rigor, objectivity and clarity.

You have released the rope which has kept you tethered to ordinary results; you are in motion and on your way.

The Secret Sauce.

In order to operate consistently and effectively, pro-urgency requires that you integrate into your belief system one simple but essential fact: virtually every decision you make can—and should—be modified, adjusted and, if necessary, revoked.

Accepting and acting on this truth in no way diminishes or requires that you change your objective. In fact, your willingness to be flexible underscores your commitment to achieving it.

Mastering pro-urgency requires a commitment to both understand and challenge your circumstances every step of the way. This is an outward manifestation that you care enough about the game-changing outcome you have selected to give it the best of your care and concern *moment-by-moment.*

A no-holds-barred evaluation of the consequences of your previous actions coupled with an ongoing, ever-vigilant assessment of the dynamic and actual conditions of your present environment will enable you to make immediate course corrections when and where needed.

Real-world feedback and your fully-conscious response to it make proactive urgency the living process it needs to be. This is the rocket fuel for maintaining your edge and momentum.

Your insistence upon reaching your objective and your embrace of real-time adaptability can remove any fear you might feel when things don't go as planned. Panic—"I'm off course! Now what do I do?"—becomes power: "I expected course adjustments would be required and I am ready to act on them."

Others may set the course and wait for results to show up in their inboxes. If you choose pro-urgency as your way of getting what you want, no part of it can be passive. There can be no dozing and no waiting. Nothing that is controllable or manageable can be left to chance. You must treat the entire course as though it matters. This is your active commitment. It matters.

Autopilot Isn't What it Seems.

Consider a passenger jet flying on autopilot. If you refer to the instruments and displays in the cockpit you'll see that the plane is headed in the right direction at the designated altitude and the appropriate speed. An aircraft on autopilot stays on course by taking into account and acting upon a continuously updated stream of information.

On autopilot, adjustments of speed, altitude, trajectory and a myriad of other factors are made in line with the most recent measurements. In some cases, data that was "fresh" only milliseconds before will be discarded in favor of that which is even more recent.

© Matthias Just

As to monitoring the pro-urgency process, even if you are relatively clear about your directional heading a small deviation can put you way off course. If you were driving or flying, and you were just two degrees off course for 500 miles, you would arrive at a location about seventeen miles from your intended destination (and potentially in the middle of a field or harbor)!⁵⁰

This is true for individuals, teams, businesses and jet planes.

Live for Course Corrections.

The autopilot analogy perfectly conveys what is required when you choose to act with pro-urgency. By definition, pro-urgency is a dynamic and adaptive process. It requires persistently challenging your decisions, incorporating new information and taking appropriate corrective action. This process should be accomplished with virtually no delay between the receipt of new information and the implementation of any shift that is indicated.

Set the course, get in motion, check the measurement and feedback mechanisms you have established and make course corrections. Continuously evaluate and deploy your assets and resources in the optimal service of your objective.

In making timely corrections and adaptations you are effectively making new decisions based on the feedback coming to your attention. Treat these decisions with the same weight as you did the original one. When acting with pro-urgency, every time you make a course correction (an adaptive decision) you improve your prospects for success.

Your vigilant assessment and course corrections will in certain ways parallel those embodied in triage in today's trauma centers, the hurry-up offense, high speed currency risk management and even walking a high wire. In each of these cases, the most recent information provides input that will enable the *next* decision to be better than the one made a moment ago. You are always acting on the best, most current information available and so you remain on course.

Almost everyone can make reasonably good decisions in a static state with a fixed environment and reliable resources. The saying goes, "Even a blind squirrel can find an acorn now and again."

But the rubber meets the road when consistently good adaptive decisions are made in a dynamic environment. And when you do this you will have become an exceptional pro-urgent warrior on your way to getting what you want.

Questions, Questions.

Proactive urgency should be viewed as *leveraged action*—the kind that gives you optimal results relative to the effort expended. Acting "urgently" without consistently assessing results and adjusting course based on the feedback garnered is simply scattered, low leverage, pedestrian effort.

During the course of many business conversations in which I participated as CEO, president or board member, I often asked the question: "Can you please remind me why we are doing this?"

The response was often along the lines of "I thought we were all clear that this was the best thing to do."

I would respond, "We were at the time, but can you explain it to me again?"

If the decision was still sound I would typically hear the kind of affirmations and reminders confirming why this was the case. If the original decision needed adjustment, the question opened the door to the needed conversation.

Peter Drucker once said, "There is surely nothing quite so useless as doing with great efficiency what should not be done at all." Continuous reassessment is key to avoiding useless action. The sooner you know that your once well-made decision no longer serves your objective as required, the sooner you can recalibrate and redirect your resources and energy in a more productive direction.

I see the question "Why are we doing this?" and the processes associated with it as essential to good business decision making for a company. It can be part of building a culture where challenging the status quo is expected *and* appreciated. Asking "Why are we doing this?" becomes a kind of cultural mantra.

How often do you need to ask it? Sometimes every day, sometimes less often. Certainly at the beginning and through the early stages it is important to monitor the process closely, so as to not fall back into old habits and ways of seeing things.

I think you will find it a great question to ask in many contexts in your life. Whether your answer affirms your current course of action or provides the opportunity for an adjustment, it is invaluable for staying on course.§§

As an owner electing to be urgent in pursuit of your most important objectives, you shift your understanding of consequences. They may have once called for labels such as "good" or "bad" (or as you will see in the next chapter "winning" or "losing"). But when you act with pro-urgency you are freed up to see *consequences as mere feedback—*opportunities to make adjustments that keep you on course with continued velocity and greater precision.

§§ See Chapter 16: *Neutralizing Fears*, for a discussion about utilizing questions as a way of breaking down fears.

The leverage of your education, training and experience will enable you to add speed and accuracy to your decisions in many situations. Engage the tools of consciousness and distinction discussed in earlier chapters and you will see even greater improvement.

Continuous corrective action is the mark of someone who owns their decisions and their life. It is the essence of pro-urgency.

Urgency Rule #14

An initial decision, no matter how good, immediately becomes a prospect for an adaptive decision based upon new inputs. Be the best challenger of your own decisions.

15

Barriers Are Openings, Hurdles Are Doors

(Adaptation and Problem Solving)

In any full-out effort to achieve something of high value, hurdles and barriers will be encountered and setbacks will occur. The measure of your commitment is your willingness to reframe such roadblocks—whether small or large, simple or complex—as opportunities to put another brick in the foundation underpinning your success.

It may be trite, but it is nevertheless true and worth repeating: "Having many difficulties perfects the being; having no difficulties ruins the being."[51] This statement is beautiful in its depth and simplicity. The more complex the challenge, the more chances you will have to "perfect your being." Your potential reward for creating value is typically in direct proportion to the degree of difficulty associated with it.

A Warrior's Mindset.

Acting with pro-urgency is a choice to be a warrior in the service of the most important things in your life. It puts you in the appropriate mindset for not only facing challenges but embracing them.

I appreciate George Carlin's rants about independent thinking. He once said,

I don't like ass kissers, flag wavers or team players. I like people who buck the system. Individualists. I often warn people: "Somewhere along the way, someone is going to tell you, 'There is no *I* in team.' What you should tell them is, 'Maybe not. But there is an *I* in independence, individuality and integrity.'"

If you find yourself unable to make the kind of deep commitments that involve the "I" words, you might be a reactor instead of an actor. It is next to impossible for pro-urgency to be initiated or sustained by victims—the defensive, reactive and stuck. It is impossible to be a warrior and a victim at the same time. If you find yourself in the latter category, you will have to challenge and ultimately abandon that way of being in order to access your full personal power.

Overcoming an attitude of victimhood frees up the strength and energy you are spending on defending the status quo and explaining the reasons why "It can't be done" or "I can't do it." When proactively engaged and applied to objectives we really care about, urgency represents the ownership of *doing*, not merely trying.

For much of what you do, there is nothing wrong with the incremental improvements to be had by "putting one foot in front of the other." In fact, with persistent effort over time this approach can represent a sure path to making progress toward your key objectives.

Along the way, though, many of your days may end with something that looks and feels a lot like ordinariness.

If you choose an objective you consider important for defining or bettering your life and the lives of those around you, accepting leisurely, incremental steps in getting there isn't going to cut it for you.

One of the benefits of acting with urgency-by-choice is your ongoing discovery of new ways to infuse your efforts with a consistent level of intensity. As a result, your days can shift from ordinary to intensely purposeful and energetic.

You must—and will want to—be a warrior in your own service. This means turning your own status quo on its head.

Rock the Boat.

Pro-urgency is manifested in part as zealous self-interest. At times you will need to free yourself from going along and getting along if it sidetracks you from what is required for your success. Such a committed approach is neither good nor bad—it is simply doing what is required.

The path of least resistance will always be crowded with those who occupy half-numb, half-lived lives. Their numbers are represented by the big, middle part of a bell curve graph. This is where you will always find the comfort zone of the collective. This, too, is where much of the not-so-thoughtful criticism of those actually pursuing their lives with vigor comes from.

A choice to act with pro-urgency comes with permission to view criticism and other forms of rock-throwing, as well as obstacles of all kinds, as *fuel* for your cause.

Umair Haque, Director of Havas Media Labs and gifted and provocative writer, writes:

> Status quo-*preserving* debates are the realm of the incrementalist. Careful and cautious, the

incrementalist's overriding concern is the past and present—not the future and certainly not possibility, exploration, or to-hell-with-it levels of Picasso-like reinvention . . . Status-quo preserving debates [only help you stay in or get] back to square one . . .

Status-quo-*disrupting* debates are concerned with getting past square one; not merely restoring a system to a previous state, but rebuilding the system for higher peaks of performance . . .[52]

Central to effective action with proactive urgency is understanding the difference between the common and uncommon. Achieving what we care about most requires daily effort to overcome the ease and consequent temptation of the common. The following quote comes from the iconoclastic American longshoreman/philosopher Eric Hoffer. I have taken the liberty of customizing his observation by substituting "pro-urgency" for the word "talent."

They who lack [pro-urgency] expect things to happen without effort. They ascribe failure to a lack of inspiration or ability, or to misfortune, rather than to insufficient application. At the core of every true [commitment to pro-urgency] there is an awareness of the difficulties inherent in any achievement, and the confidence that by persistence and patience something worthwhile will be realized. Thus [pro-urgency] is a species of vigor.[53]

No matter whether you are a physical laborer, an athlete or entertainer, a homemaker, business person, astronaut or fisherman, your mindset can be a differentiating factor in how you live your life—especially when you choose to pursue an objective with conscious urgency.

Moments of Truth.

Moments of truth is a concept that is very simple yet applicable in virtually all environments and situations. It offers a way to approach the hurdles and roadblocks that mark the path of everything worth doing with the best of your personal power.

Every day you confront people, situations and decision points where an opportunity is presented to maintain or accelerate the velocity of your pro-urgent effort. These kinds of encounters also hold the potential to halt your progress— or even send you backward. The way you engage yourself and others in these moments of truth determines whether they become entry points for problem solving and forward motion or missed opportunities.

What are your options when you are face-to-face with an opportunity masquerading as an obstacle? Let's address them in terms of attitudes conveyed and impressions left.

> ➤ The first one is "Scorched Earth." Here you purposefully or without thinking infuse the situation with negativity. You leave a poor impression of yourself, your product or services. Your actions make the moment truly memorable for yourself and for the others present—in a bad way. You alienate rather than engage. You take or hurt, rather than give or serve. You withhold your best rather than offering it up with gratitude for the opportunity to share it. Essentially, you manage to turn a speed bump into a barrier. The end result when the dust settles? There was a moment of truth alright—and you lost. The obstacle remains firmly in place and the goal more distant.

➤ The second approach is "Do No Harm." This is where most of us fall short. Here you don't eviscerate the moment like you do using the "Scorched Earth" approach, but neither do you seize it. In this kind of interaction you may as well not be present. You create no impression and nobody cares that you don't. You are passive and watching rather than active and engaged. Not only do you withhold your best, you don't offer anything at all. You leave the opportunity to create a positive experience without even recognizing it was there. The only silver lining is that even though you didn't advance your cause, at least you didn't leave a bad impression. The obstacle remains and the finish line hasn't moved.

➤ The third approach is "Winning." Here you recognize and embrace the opportunity for overcoming a hurdle through proactivity. You bring your "A-Game" and make certain that the person or situation benefits from your presence and attention. You offer your best in the moment, without thought of return. You recognize that an essential foundation principle for acting with pro-urgency is to ask and answer the questions: "How can I help and how can I serve? How can I leave this challenge with a solution (or at least the start of one) and turn an apparent barrier into a doorway?"

You are actively engaged and highly aware. You eliminate distractions and treat the subject of your interaction as if in all the world only they matter. You create with them and leave the moment, situation and person better than before. As a result, you (or your company, service or product) are remembered with favor and for creating goodwill. In short, you take the moment and convert it into something that serves you, your objective and those along the path to it. You "win" the moment of truth. The obstacle itself is either removed or changed as a result of your approach and interaction. It may require additional effort to overcome or eliminate it, but you have had a positive impact.

In an organization, powerful change can be created by people coming together around the idea of winning thousands of moments of truth in the next year—maybe even the next *month*. Make a personal and collective commitment to stack up piles and piles of positive impressions and contributions. Consider them defining mileposts where you make the choice to "win" the moment and not leave it unattended or lost. Leave a trail of these moments and you overcome obstacles and win with your customers, co-workers, family and friends. Serve others *and* your organization on a collective journey with proactive urgency.

The Signposts Will Appear.

Acting with pro-urgency will bring you face-to-face with the challenges that are part and parcel of achieving something special. You will experience missteps and backsliding. But if you stay in motion, answers—or at least the signposts and clues as to your next step—will always appear.

I have repeatedly used the words "edge" and "commitment" and "intention" and "intensity." These are words tied to action. There is an obvious distinction between being proactive and passive. You see examples of the manifestation of each in every situation you encounter. Individual DNA may have some role in how each of us acts, but for the most part *we are owners or victims by decision*— or by default if we choose *not* to choose.

Whether you are young or old, female or male, rich or poor, able-bodied or infirm, aggressive or passive, choosing ownership—*on your terms*—engages the passionate edge that underlies any successful pro-urgent effort.

A mindful warrior chooses ownership, with pro-urgency as the weapon of choice.

Urgency Rule #15

Challenges and hurdles define the path of proactive urgency. Seek out and win moments of truth as a way of building and maintaining your momentum.

16

Neutralizing Fears

(**A**lleviating Fears)

In the pursuit of most objectives of importance, your course, velocity and ability to commit are impacted by a virtually endless stream of fears.

What would you do and what would you let go of in this moment if you knew that a goal you were fearful of pursuing today would not be an option tomorrow?

If you are an excellent procrastinator, you would immediately begin yet another conversation with yourself about why that couldn't really be true, and why there is always another day, and why if you wait a while it will probably be a better day at that.

But could fooling yourself with a belief that the opportunity has only limited availability help you reframe your fear into a thief? A thief stealing your time and potential adventures and your very life force away from you? If your fear was stealing all of your opportunities, could you confront it?

For all we know, many of the opportunities available to you at the moment may no longer be around after today. Certainly this would be true if circumstances conspired to make this particular day the one where you draw your last breath. In less extreme terms, picture someone else preempting your opportunity—or seizing it for themselves—if you don't move on it today.

Fear is a thief.

Pro-urgency does not require the absence of fears. If a state of "no fear" was a requirement for the achievement of anything of note, nothing would ever happen. Fears are and always will be a part of the landscape.

In my own experience, moving through fears requires a shift from avoiding them to direct and pragmatic exposure of their weaknesses.

"Sunlight is the best disinfectant." This well-known expression was authored by U.S. Supreme Court Justice Louis Brandeis. It was first mentioned in a letter to his fiancé in 1891. He wrote, "If the broad light of day could be let in upon men's actions, it would purify them as the sun disinfects."[54] Letting the light in is a good metaphor for how to clean out the fears that hold you back.

Questioning Fears.

Within the construct of all fears there are falsehoods masquerading as truth. For this reason, I believe that questions have a lot of value as part of an approach to neutralize them. The answers can be important too, but by asking enough questions you will be *challenging and engaging the fear* rather than leaving it undisturbed and at full strength. With the right kinds of questions, you will likely be able to expose the fear for the absurdity that it often turns out to be.

My mentor and friend Larry Wilson directly and indirectly taught tens of thousands of salespeople, executives, teams and individuals about dealing with fears. He observed, "The opportunity for success is often derailed by fear. It's actually not the feeling of fear; it's the avoidance of fear. We think we are protecting ourselves in the name of safety, but we simply don't play the game to win it."[55]

We typically cloak our fears with a strength and unassailability they do not deserve. When we question our fears instead of simply reacting to them or remaining passive, we create an opportunity to expose their weaknesses. Doing this enables us to step in the direction of diminishing them or neutralizing them altogether.

For example, when you are fearful of being wrong, you might start by asking some of the following questions:

> ➢ Is it more important for me to be right or to avoid being wrong?
>
> ➢ Other than how it might make me *feel*, what are the consequences of being wrong?
>
> ➢ What is worse: being wrong, or not acting because I am afraid of being wrong?
>
> ➢ What if I didn't even use the labels right and wrong and viewed the outcome simply as feedback?

Asking these questions—or almost any others that are relevant—shifts the issue away from the thought "I'm afraid" toward "Let me understand what is really happening here." Ask yourself more questions like these and you will move beyond emotion-based anxiety in the direction of the kind of rational inquiry that will help you more realistically address, and perhaps alleviate, the fear.

Let's consider the fear of taking that important first step outside our comfort zones. Sooner or later, we must all advance beyond those boundaries. This can lead to an immediate confrontation with emotional discomfort. If you make a commitment to anticipating and embracing that discomfort as mere feedback on the journey to getting what you want, these and similar questions may help you get started:

> ➤ What about the situation made me emotionally uncomfortable? Why?

> ➤ Did the anxiety or embarrassment I experienced in that particular situation really matter a week or a month later? Does it matter in the context of my whole life?

> ➤ What action could I have taken to eliminate or at least reduce the anxiety I felt?

> ➤ What did I miss out on or didn't get resolved because I chose to avoid the discomfort by not moving from my comfortable perch?

Again, keep asking yourself questions like these and it is likely you will gradually focus less and less on your emotional discomfort and more on understanding the boundaries of your comfort zone and how to move past them. If you are in the process of challenging the fear in the form of questions—you cannot be mired in it any longer. You're too busy!

Remember, too, that the art and science of asking questions improves (as does everything else) with practice. Keep at it, and you will start making short work of many of the fears that threaten to hold you back.

"Is It True?"

A terrific system using questions to address fears has been developed by author and teacher Byron Katie. It is one of the most direct, pragmatic and rapid ways for confronting the fears that may be preventing you from taking action or utilizing the best of your potential—or from anything else for that matter. She says, "I don't let go of concepts—I question them. Then *they* let go of *me*." Her approach to discovering the truth about your fears is in complete alignment with proactive urgency.

She suggests starting by writing down the fear you are confronting with as much specificity as you can. Include why you think it came up when, where and how it did. Once you have done so, the first question to ask yourself is "Is it true?" You can respond with "yes" or "no," but explain your answer in as much detail as you can muster. How do you *know* the fear is "true?" Write it down.

Then ask the second question—which is a more urgent version of the first one. Because it is unlikely that you have sufficiently challenged what is behind the fear with your answer to the first question, now ask, "Can you *absolutely know* it's true?" What points can you cite as actual proof for its existence and validity in your world? Hopefully, with this extra nudge, you will begin to see cracks in the façade of your fear.

Be specific. Articulate the facts that have led you to the conclusion that the fear is not merely conjured by you, but is a real affront underpinned by verifiable facts.

Which part of it *might* be true? Which part may need to be qualified? What part, if any, simply isn't true at all? How can I know? Write it down.

Below I offer an example of Ms. Katie's approach to cracking the hold that fear had on one woman.[56] This is an illustration of how it is possible to rapidly—almost immediately—transform your perspective with just a few questions. What follows is an actual dialogue between Byron

Katie and Caitlin Flanagan[57], a writer then suffering with Stage IV breast cancer.

Ms. Flanagan first related to Katie the details of her cancer, how her diagnosis was very poor, and how she had two small children who needed her. She told Katie that she believed her children needed her so much that she feared for *their* survival should she die. She found the chemo exhausting and had no idea if the treatment was going to work. Here is what happened next in their conversation.

> Katie: Your children need you. Is that true?
>
> Flanagan: Yes! They're nine years old! They're little boys! They just finished fourth grade!
>
> Katie: Uh-huh. Your children need you—is that true?
>
> Flanagan: Yes, it's true! My children obviously need me.
>
> Katie: Where are they right now?
>
> Flanagan: They're with their dad, my husband.
>
> Katie: Is he good with the boys?
>
> Flanagan: Oh, yeah, he is the best dad in the *world,* and he does so much with them, and the three of them have a great relationship—you cannot imagine. He should get dad of the year.
>
> Katie: Your children need you. Is that true?
>
> Flanagan, to herself: *I just sat there and sat there and sat there—and then* kaboom *in my mind like you cannot believe: I realized that Katie had nailed it. It wasn't the cancer, or the chemo, or the baldness that was keeping me in hell—it was the terror of thinking that if I didn't make it, my boys wouldn't either. But they would. They would! If, in fact, I didn't make it, my boys would be okay. Their*

dad would take care of them. And all our relatives. And everyone at church. They'd be fine. They could and would make it without me if they had to.

Katie: That's right, sweetheart, how narcissistic to think they couldn't live if you didn't live.

This dialogue involves a real and present threat of death by cancer. It is quite confrontational—even somewhat brutal. Consider what it would be like to apply this type of challenge to your own fears. They may be lesser or greater than the fear Ms. Flanagan was confronting. They all are capable of being exposed for the lies they represent.[58]

If your fears are stealing your life from you, isn't it worth being confrontational? Shine a bright light on them. Question them. Examine the thoughts and feelings you have *about* them.

Consider the simplicity of the questions: "Is it true?" and "Can you absolutely know that it is true?" Could it be any easier to open the door to parting ways with your fears? Courage, of course, is required. Courage to ask questions, and courage to not accept the first superficial answers that come to mind.

Many of us choose to make dealing with fear a lot harder than it needs to be. It comes down to a choice: You can choose to keep your fears strapped to your back. Or you can set them down and cross-examine them until you get a confession: "I give up! I don't really exist as truth!" You can leave them behind and press on ahead without the extra weight associated with giving them energy and attention *they almost never really deserve.*

Another Way Forward: Staying in Motion.

Some species of sharks—including the great white, the mako and the whale shark—have to keep moving to breathe. This is the only way to bring fresh oxygen into their bodies. If these sharks stop moving, they die.

Consider what happens when we feel paralyzed by fear. Anxiety reduces the amount of oxygen coming into our system. Less oxygen puts a bigger strain on our bodies and amplifies feelings of anxiety. We find ourselves in the middle of a self-defeating loop where we need to move past our fear—but it is robbing us of the energy we need to do it.

Thomas Watson, Jr., longtime Chairman and CEO of IBM, had a bias for action, believing that a decision to act is never wrong. He wrote, "Doing nothing is a comfortable alternative [to action] because it is without risk, but it is an absolutely fatal way to manage a business." I would add that it is also a self-defeating way to live your life.

Motion infuses our efforts with oxygen, providing continuous, dynamic feedback. Inertia doesn't. When we are busy—actively in motion—we have less time and inclination to pay attention to and feed our fears. If we choose passivity when confronted with fear, we will find ourselves gasping for air. When we *act* we gain fresh energy, perspectives and oxygen with which we can neutralize and move past our fears.

For our purposes, recognize that fears can and will show up in any work you drive with your version of proactive urgency. But as you learn to habitually question and move past them, you can reduce them from barriers to speed bumps—and maybe even clear the road of some of them altogether.

I remind you of the quote from Buddha: "There are only two mistakes one can make along the road to truth; not going all the way, and not starting."

Urgency Rule #16

Neutralize the fears that will attempt to block your path. Take the mask off fear masquerading as truth by challenging its legitimacy.

17

<u>Your Personal Imprint</u>

(All In.)

Embracing pro-urgency is a way of increasing your intensity and sense of purpose for achieving the things you have decided can be game-changing for you. Whether in your work or in the engagement that is your full life, acting with pro-urgency could not be a more personal effort.

Dick Wagner is a lifelong rock musician, songwriter, arranger and author.[59] He is also a good friend. He wrote songs and played lead guitar with Alice Cooper for many years. He also spent part of his on-stage and in-studio career with Aerosmith, Kiss, Lou Reed and Peter Gabriel, among many others.

Dragoo Photography

He told me that the same guitar played by a master musician will produce tones different from those made by any other person picking up and playing the same instrument.

"A practiced ear can distinguish between the tones produced by me versus Stevie Ray Vaughn, playing the same piece of music on the same guitar. A trained listener will be able to recognize, 'That's Dick Wagner playing the solos on *Texas Flood*, or that's Stevie Ray.'"

He also said, "The difference is not in the music as written or in the instrument. The distinction is in how the body of the artist is connected to the instrument, the strength or softness of how it is cradled, the player's posture and even the angle of the fingers striking the strings. It is also a function of the level of consciousness and emotion applied to creating the music."

The music charts don't make the difference. The instrument and amplification don't make the difference, and neither do the wardrobe or the venue. It is the artist's personal imprint that creates the uniqueness, and everyone in the audience knows it. It is personal and that's why each person is there.

The process of acting with proactive urgency is like this. It is personal. It is yours to create for yourself—to customize. It is yours to play unlike anyone else in the world. It is not surprising that the skills that will make pro-urgency work for you are, in your area of uniqueness, the same kind that distinguish a professional performer from an ordinary player. A master musician from an apprentice.

How will you know you are fully engaged with pro-urgency? It will be personal.

- ➤ You will be fully committed to the process at hand.
- ➤ You will be giving the best of yourself to everything associated with your effort.
- ➤ You will be entirely clear about your objective and why it matters.
- ➤ You won't care how much time you must devote to achieving your objective. You may not even notice.
- ➤ You will see problems and challenges as hurdles or doorways, not barriers.
- ➤ You will be creating with what you have—not waiting for what you don't.
- ➤ You will be actively engaging people in your effort.
- ➤ You will openly question and neutralize the fears that come up.
- ➤ You will be in the process of getting what you want.

As stated earlier, the power of urgency is always present and immediately accessible. When harnessed with clarity of intention and commitment in the service of your most important goals, it is a force with which you can create almost immediate transformation.

It simply isn't necessary to wait for a crisis or emergency to offer your best in your own service and in the service of others.

Urgency Rule #17

Proactive urgency is personal. If pursued with clarity and commitment, it will transform your work, your life and the lives of those around you.

About the Author

William Keiper wrote *The Power of Urgency* as an expression of what he has learned and accomplished applying urgency in his work and life. His mission in life is motivation, leadership and support for businesses and individuals committed to the urgent pursuit and achievement of their important objectives.

He has served as Chairman of the Board, Chief Executive Officer, President and trusted advisor for a variety of public and private companies, and committed individuals. Through his consulting firm FirstGlobal® Partners, Mr. Keiper serves individuals, company owners, executives, investors and others in situations where the status quo will no longer be tolerated.

He earned a business degree with honors from Eastern Illinois University, a law degree from the Sandra Day O'Connor College of Law at Arizona State University, and a Master's degree from the Thunderbird School of Global Management.

In addition to *The Power of Urgency*, he is the award-winning and best-selling author of *LIFE Expectancy: It's Never Too Late to Change Your Game* and *Apple for President!*

The Power of Urgency

Stories from the Front Lines

A message from Will:

Dear Reader,

I have in the works a follow-up book offering examples of proactive urgency in action. These stories inspire all of us to aim high and not be denied our most important goals.

Whether in a business or a personal context, I would love to hear your story of the power of your engagement with purposeful urgency. If you would enjoy sharing it, please contact me directly at:

will@firstglobalpartners.com

Thank-you for reading *The Power of Urgency.*

William Keiper

The Urgency Rules

1. Proactive urgency is purposeful, insistent, committed action pursued with a passionate edge. It is an activist choice to access your deepest personal power for the creation of almost immediate transformation.

2. It is your choice to act with "first responder" urgency outside of an emergency or a crisis. Pro-urgency is a powerful way to engage your highest and best resources to get what you want.

3. Urgency-by-choice is the province of the active, directed and decisive mind. Your engagement of proactive urgency will be evident from the level of your commitment to the objective, the attentiveness and depth of your focus, the velocity and timeliness of your actions, the fierceness of your pursuit. Engage it in the service of objectives that will be game-changing in your work and your life.

4. The world has changed. Our long-trusted external support systems are weakening. Self-reliance in thought and action is critical for reaching your most important objectives.

5. Take an inventory of your personal strengths and weaknesses. You will find that in apparent weakness lies amazing personal power. Permit the awareness of the finite nature of your life to fuel your personal urgency.

6. Choosing to act with on-demand urgency yields continuous, incremental advantages. Think of pro-urgency as your edge in a competition—*your life*—where winning by fractions always matters.

7. As an organizational leader at any level, commit yourself and your associates to a single important objective to pursue with proactive urgency and a passionate edge—starting now. Your formula for success: 80%-plus confidence-level decisions with continuous monitoring and timely correction.

8. Your purposeful urgency can be fueled by the knowledge and sensory awareness you command at all levels of consciousness. Learn to rely upon your *sense of things* in addition to what you can objectively verify.

9. There is power, clarity and efficiency in creating and consciously attending to distinctions. You can see what you need to see, when you need to see it.

10. The future of a moment ago has arrived. You bring to it your perfection along with your uniqueness. Make it your mission to leverage your uniqueness starting immediately.

11. Security is mainly illusory. Remember Helen Keller's words: "Avoiding danger is typically no safer in the long run than outright exposure." Practice leaving your comfort zone.

12. A purposeful commitment to acting with pro-urgency is a sustained, continuously renewed promise manifested in your bold actions. This ongoing promise leaves no room for fakery, conformity or false consensus.

13. Set your goal to pursue with proactive urgency with as much clarity and descriptiveness as you can. Be ruthlessly objective in assessing the totality of the environment and conditions that exist at the starting

line for your effort. Gather, review and digest all of the information that is available.

14. An initial decision, no matter how good, immediately becomes a prospect for an adaptive decision based upon new inputs. Be the best challenger of your own decisions.

15. Challenges and hurdles define the path of proactive urgency. Seek out and win moments of truth as a way of building and maintaining your momentum.

16. Neutralize the fears that will attempt to block your path. Take the mask off fear masquerading as truth by challenging its legitimacy.

17. Proactive urgency is personal. If pursued with clarity and commitment, it will transform your work, your life and the lives of those around you.

The Power of Urgency: {#unnumbered}
The "A-Game" System {#unnumbered}

1. **A**ctive Commitment.

2. **A**bsolute Truth.

3. **A**ssessment and Continuous Adjustments.

4. **A**daptation and Problem Solving.

5. **A**lleviating Fears.

6. **A**ll In.

Endnotes

Chapter 1: High Wire, No Rope

[1] The story of this adventure is told in the documentary film: *Man on Wire*, directed by James Marsh (2008; Magnolia Home Entertainment).

[2] "Passion," Urban Dictionary, accessed June 1, 2013. www.urbandictionary.com/define.php?term=passion

Chapter 2: Reactive Urgency – Fight or Flight

[3] Layton, Julie. "How Fear Works," howstuffworks, accessed June 1, 2013.
http://science.howstuffworks.com/life/fear2.htm

[4] Selye, Hans. *Stress without distress*. Philadelphia: J.B. Lippincott Company, 1974.

[5] He offered examples of such things as meeting a non-threatening challenge, engaging in physical exercise and sports, and even gambling.

[6] Frankenhauser, M., T. M. Dembroski, T. H. Schmidt, & G. Blumchen. eds. *Biobehavioral Bases of Coronary Heart Disease*. New York: Plenum Press, 1983.

[7] Not his real name.

[8] Federal Bureau of Investigation. *Violent Encounters*. Washington D.C.: U.S. Department of Justice. 2006. [Emphasis added.] *Note:* In this quote, reducing the "non-adaptive effects of evolution" refers to the potential neutralization of the flight-or flight response that might otherwise come up for the first responder, in order to make room for an appropriate, learned response.

Chapter 3: The Sense in Urgency

9 Covey, Stephen. *The Seven Habits of Highly Effective People: Powerful Lessons in Personal Change.* New York: Free Press, 1989.

Covey, Stephen. *First Things First.* Great Britain, UK: Simon and Schuster, 1994.

10 Eric Hoffer (July 25, 1902–May 21, 1983) was an American moral and social philosopher.

11 "Defriend: A term stemming from the internet social network crowd, meaning to remove someone from a list of friends. The term is misleading because usually neither of you were friends to begin with. "Defriending" is essentially a way of cutting off already useless communication with cyber-people." Urban Dictionary, accessed June 1, 2013. http://www.urbandictionary.com/define.php?term=defriend

12 Vinod Kholsa interview on April 24, 2002. In Seelig, Tina. *What I Wish I Knew When I Was 20: A Crash Course on Making Your Place in the World.* New York: HarperOne, 2009.

Chapter 4: Self-Reliance – Now More Than Ever

13 Centers for Disease Control and Prevention, National Vital Statistics System, accessed June 19, 2013. http://www.cdc.gov/nchs/mardiv.htm

14 The ultimate incarnation of this was the "company town," memorialized in Hardy Green's 2010 book, *The Company Town: The Industrial Edens and Satanic Mills That Shaped the American Economy.*

[15] College Board Advocacy & Policy Center. Trends in College Pricing. 2012. Accessed June 21, 2013.
http://trends.collegeboard.org/college-pricing

[16] Chaves, Mark. "The Decline of American Religion?" *ARDA Guiding Paper Series*. State College, PA: The Association of Religion Data Archives at The Pennsylvania State University, 2011.
http://www.thearda.com/rrh/papers/guidingpapers/Chaves.asp
See also: Chaves, Mark. *American Religion: Contemporary Trends*. New Jersey: Princeton University Press, 2011.

[17] Note that I am not making a value judgment regarding any particular belief (or lack thereof), only pointing out facts that suggest traditional religion in America once served as a more important touchstone for a larger percentage of the population.

[18] Saad, Lydia. "U.S. Confidence in Religion at Low Point." Gallup Politics, Jul 12, 2012, accessed June 20, 2013.
http://www.gallup.com/poll/155690/confidence-organized-religion-low-point.aspx

[19] Worthen, Molly. "One Nation Under God?" *New York Times Sunday Review,* December 22, 2012.

[20] Ovans, Andrea. "Capturing the Upside of Risk." HBR Blog Network, June 27, 2012, accessed June 2, 2013.
http://blogs.hbr.org/cs/2012/06/capturing_the_upside_of_risk.html

Chapter 5: Discovering Personal Urgency

[21] Consult any actuarial table, e.g.:
http://gosset.wharton.upenn.edu/mortality/perl/CalcForm.html

[22] Keiper, William. *Life Expectancy: It's Never Too Late to Change Your Game.* FirstGlobalPartners LLC, 2012.

[23] One of his books is *Uncertainty: Turning Fear and Doubt into Fuel for Brilliance.* His blog can be found at http://www.jonathanfields.com/blog/

[24] Fields, Jonathan. "Dust in the Wind?" accessed Apr 10, 2013, http://www.jonathanfields.com/blog/was-this-your-life/

Chapter 6: A 1% Advantage

[25] Personal communication with the author.

Chapter 7: The Pro-Urgent Business

[26] Zook, Chris. "When 'Creative Destruction' Destroys More than It Creates." HBR Blog Nework, June 27, 2012, accessed June 2, 2013.
http://blogs.hbr.org/cs/2012/06/when_creative_destructio n_dest.html
Chris Zook is co-author, with James Allen, of *Repeatability: Build Enduring Businesses for a World of Constant Change.*

[27] Shill W, Engel JF, Mann D, Schatteman O. "Corporate Agility–Six Ways to Make Volatility Your Friend." *Accenture Outlook,* No. 3, 2012. Accessed June 2, 2013.
http://www.accenture.com/us-en/outlook/Pages/outlook-journal-2012-corporate-agility-six-ways-to-make-volatility-your-friend.aspx

[28] Twelve-point agility checklist (*Ibid.*):

1. Does your organization have at least three scenarios for how your industry is most likely to evolve over the next 36 months? Does it have good options for responding?

2. What three big opportunities would your company be pursuing if it were more agile?

3. Imagine three possible sources of competition that you haven't thought would be likely until now. How will you respond to them?

4. Put yourself in your top competitors' shoes. What could they do to disrupt the market in the next year, and what are your plans for outsmarting them?

5. How is your company augmenting its ability to quickly sense new market anomalies? Are you taking full advantage of the new capabilities of today's analytics tools?

6. What are the three biggest factors preventing your organization from being more agile? How do you plan to overcome them?

7. Did you make such big cuts during the recession (particularly in terms of talent) that your agility and ability to grow have been damaged? If so, how are you compensating now for those cuts?

8. In what areas should you be collaborating with your competitors to drive changes in the market?

9. Who among your organization's new leaders will be most effective at taking advantage of volatility? What makes them different from your longtime leaders?

10. Which of your customers are the best leading indicators of future market opportunities?

11. Where would faster decision making be of most benefit to your company?

12. Have you been able to cut your company's fixed costs in the past few years to improve its agility?

29 See, *Faster Cheaper Better: The 9 Levers for Transforming How Work Gets Done* by Michael Hammer and Lisa Hershman.

30 First mover advantage describes "a form of competitive advantage that a company earns by being the first to enter a specific market or industry. Being the first allows a company to acquire superior brand recognition, client loyalty and market share. The company also has more time to perfect its product or service." (a) When a first-mover is not able to capitalize on its advantage, the opportunity can be available for "other firms to compete effectively and efficiently versus the earlier entrants. These individuals then gain a second-mover advantage." (b) Read more here: (a) "First Mover." Investopedia, accessed June 2, 2013. http://www.investopedia.com/terms/f/firstmover.asp#ixzz2 LCgvCdKU
(b) "First Mover Advantage." Wikipedia, accessed June 2, 2013. http://en.wikipedia.org/wiki/First-mover_advantage

31 Shill W, et al. "Corporate Agility–Six Ways to Make Volatility Your Friend."

32 The name FiREapps is an extended acronym for "Financial Risk Exposed."

33 FiREapps Corporate Earnings Currency Impact Report looked at 794 companies that had at least $450 million in revenue with 15% or more coming internationally in at least two currencies. Only 23 companies reported currency-related gains, compared with the 205 that experienced negative effects.

Chapter 8: Consciousness – You Know What You Need to Know

34 Wilson AD and Golonka S. "Embodied cognition is not what you think it is." *Front. Psychology* **4**:58. 2013.

35 Erhard W. "A Breakthrough in Individual and Social Transformation." *The Eranos Foundation*. Presentation at the Eranos Conference, Ascona, Switzerland 18 June 2006

36 In the next chapter I bring to your attention the use of distinctions as a way to separate things that are relevant for your current interest from those that are not. Employing the power of distinctions along with the deliberate use of the methods discussed above can—with surprising ease— improve your ability to be pro-urgent with a high degree of confidence and no waiting.

37 Some call this the "super-conscious mind." "By impressing your goals upon your subconscious mind, your super-conscious will respond accordingly, you will just not know exactly how . . . Subconsciously, you will attract certain situations and resources [for your use]."
@dieselpokers. "The Superconscious Mind." Zazenlife.com. March 1, 2012. Accessed June 2, 2013.
http://zazenlife.com/2012/03/01/super-conscious-mind/

38 "Distinction." Wiktionary, accessed June 2, 2013.
http://simple.wiktionary.org/wiki/distinction

39 Jonathan Swift (1667–1745), author of *Gulliver's Travels*.

Chapter 12: Acts, Not Words – Commitment and Authenticity

40 Keller, Helen. *The Open Door*. New York: Doubleday, 1957.

[41] Argyris, Chris. Teaching Smart People How to Learn (Harvard Review Business Classics). Connecticut: Harvard Business School Press, 2008.

[42] Erhard W, Jensen M. "The Three Foundations of a Great Life, Great Leadership, and a Great Organization." Social Science Research Network, August 5, 2011, accessed June 2, 2013. http://ssrn.com/abstract=1850544
Michael Jensen is the Jessie Isidor Strauss Professor Emeritus, Harvard Business School and Chairman, Social Science Research Network, Inc.

[43] Not his real name.

[44] Grove, Andy. *Only the Paranoid Survive: How to Exploit the Crisis Points That Challenge Every Company.* New York: Currency Books. 1999.

Chapter 13: What Is True?

[45] This material merely scratches the surface of what goal-setting is and how it should be accomplished. There are many quality resources for this aspect of your effort. The following blog entry from August 2011, "The Top 10 Online Goal Setting and Tracking Tools," by C.D. Crowder, refers to a number of online tools as examples. (Accessed June 4, 2013.)
http://voices.yahoo.com/the-top-10-online-goal-setting-tracking-tools-9037665.html?cat=15
Here also is an article that debunks goal setting in favor of real transformation: Williams, Ray B. "Why Goal Setting Doesn't Work." Psychology Today: Wired for Success, April 11, 2011, accessed June 4, 2013.
http://www.psychologytoday.com/blog/wired-success/201104/why-goal-setting-doesnt-work

[46] See, for example, *In Extremis Leadership: Leading As If Your Life Depended On It*, by Thomas A. Kolditz.